WHA
ARE

If anyone is qualified t ⎯⎯⎯⎯ ⎯ope it's my good friend David Peters. I ⎯⎯ ⎯⎯ known David and his lovely wife Jane for many years and have seen in them both a tested and unwavering faith ... a faith that is fueled by an undying hope that is founded upon the surest thing on this earth – the promises of a God who cannot lie. Their lives stand as a contradiction to the unbiblical promise of modern Christianity to a deeply troubled world – that God has a "wonderful" plan for their lives, and that plan is one of smooth sailing, filled with tranquility and true happiness. The truth is that we enter the Kingdom of God through much tribulation. As you follow David and Jane through turbulent storms in an ocean of troubles, you will grow in the hope that is an anchor of the soul, both sure and steadfast.

— Ray Comfort, Author, Co-host of "The Way of the Master," Los Angeles, California, USA.

You can only give what you have. I have known David and Jane Peters for decades and they truly have great hope that has grown out of very difficult circumstances. Through this book you will receive fresh hope and your hope will be restored and strengthened. You will gain a whole new level of understanding of the power of hope in your life. This book will truly inspire and encourage you. It is a must read for 21st century living.

— Clinton Kelleher, Senior Minister, Cathedral of Hope, Christchurch, New Zealand

David Peters writes about hope from his unique perspective – not as a spectator, but part way through a grueling race that would test the most resolute spiritual athlete. I thought I had already learned a lot about hope from knowing David and Jane and their incredibly brave journey over several years: now, this book gives me an even richer understanding about a most precious quality. If faith tested by fire is what we aspire to, let's make sure we also learn about hope tested in the storms. David Peters has such hope, and he has gifted us a series of precious personal insights."

— Rob Harley,
Writer and Journalist, Auckland, New Zealand

This book describes a journey, full of gripping vignettes and colourful, illustrative personal stories which render to us the wonderful value of hope. Hope deferred makes a heart grow sick, but hope fulfilled is the fullness of joy! Hardship, disappointment, struggle, suffering and rejection are part of life's journey, endured by Christ our Leader and part of the Way. But in this book, David masterfully brings the reader to realize they have permission to dream and wonder again. This is an honest portrayal of the pains and pleasures of life. I recommend this book to all earnest, seeking Christians who wish to follow in the footsteps of their Master.

— Robert I. Holmes, Founder/Director,
Storm Harvest Ministries, Cootamundra, Australia

HOPE

Finding the Doorway to Fulfilled Desires

By
David Peters

Published by:
CSN Books
(866) 495-7633
CSNBooks.com

Cover image by PhotoNewZealand/Forest Smyth.

Cover design by Jon Clist.

Unless otherwise indicated, all Scripture quotations are taken from the Holy Bible, New Living Translation, copyright ©1996. Used by permission of Tyndale House Publishers, Inc., Wheaton, Illinois 60189. All rights reserved.

Scripture marked NIV is taken from the HOLY BIBLE, NEW INTERNATIONAL VERSION, copyright ©1973, 1978, 1984 International Bible Society. Used by permission of Zondervan Bible Publishers.

Scripture marked RSV is taken from the REVISED STANDARD VERSION OF THE BIBLE, Old Testament section, copyright ©1952, New Testament section, copyright ©1946, by Division of Christian Education of the National Council of the Churches of Christ in the United States of America.

Scripture marked KJV is taken from the Fourth Edition of the Thompson's Chain Reference Bible, KING JAMES VERSION copyright ©1964, B.B. Kirkbride Bible Co., Inc

Scripture marked NKJV is taken The Spirit-Filled Life Bible, NEW KING JAMES VERSION, copyright ©1991, Thomas Nelson Inc.

Scripture marked Amplified is taken from THE AMPLIFIED BIBLE, copyright ©1965 by Zondervan Publishing House.

Printed in the United States of America.

DEDICATION

To Jesus Christ, my Lord and friend, whose love and grace continually amazes me.

"You were his enemies, separated from him by your evil thoughts and actions, yet now he has brought you back as his friends. He has done this through his death on the cross in his own human body" (Colossians 1:21b-22a).

ACKNOWLEDGMENTS

I would like to thank Suong-Hong Eyou, who years ago wrote an impassioned letter urging me to put my wife's and my story in written form. You were the spark that started it all.

Thank you to my ministry board – Peter Angell, Keith Fox, Doug and Beryl Maskell, Barry Thom (and previously David Lyle Morris and PhilWarbrick). Your friendship, love and input over many years have been priceless.

Thank you to our intercessory team of Peter Angell, Karen Blakely, Merrilyn Jackson, Jeanne Hill and Rachel McQueen. Your prayers and timely words of encouragement have strengthened Jane and me repeatedly.

Craig Heilmann, my Aussie mate, you are a wonderful theologian and author. Your editorial advice has been invaluable.

Thanks to Murray Thom, producer of the Piano by Candlelight, Together, and Miracle projects. Your design tips have been helpful, especially the comment, "When you think its good, you can do better." I hope we have done that comment justice.

Jon Clist – thanks for your graphics work and especially your patience when I kept changing my mind!

Thanks to Paul Restall and Felicity Peters for help with the photographic work. You are much appreciated family members.

Allison Moss – thanks so much for putting the draft manuscript into paper form.

Thank you to Grant Crary and the team at Christian Services Network for accepting the manuscript and seeing it through to print. It has been a pleasure to work with you.

Thank you to all the wonderful leaders and members of my home church. Your help, love and acceptance have blessed Jane and me so much.

Thanks to my awesome sons – Joe, Adam, Tim, wonderful daughter-in-law Katherine, and precious grandchildren Jordan and Charlotte – you have made us feel blessed to be parents. This book is your story too.

Finally, thank you to my courageous wife Jane, whose beautiful smile, despite her circumstances, says more than a book ever can.

FOREWORD

David Peters has written a book that cuts to the core of an issue that is central to the heart of God. I predict that you will be touched deeply and moved spiritually.

Do you need hope and encouragement? This is a book for those who feel overwhelmed with the complexity of our times. In David we have a proven leader, a modern Joshua who can show us the way. I appreciate the opportunity to learn from a man of vast experience who has overcome heartbreaking obstacles, yet there is much more here than instruction about the individual's pathway to survival and contentment.

David has gathered together a treasure-trove of insights for today's spiritual leader. Drawing from deep streams of personal revelation, honoring the lessons of church history and integrated with the great teachings of the scripture, this book is a valuable reference for emerging leaders seeking to guide ministries and congregations into the future. Full of gripping personal stories that made me weep and worship, I was encouraged and instructed by the great wisdom set down in these pages.

David and his family are a shining example to us of perseverance, patience, faithfulness and courage. You will have to discover the remarkable content of this book for yourself, however I long for you to know David personally as I do because the actions of a true shepherd always speak louder than their words.

He is a veteran Christian leader, characterized by dignity, humility, strength of resolve, love, and humor, who lives to honor the good in others. He and his family radiate the beauty of Jesus. Every Christian should read this book – a sensitively discussed, but starkly honest guide through the pains and pleasures of life.

John Dawson,
President, Youth with a Mission

INTRODUCTION

"May the God of hope fill you with all joy and peace,
As you trust in him;
So that you may overflow with hope,
By the power of the Holy Spirit."[1]

Overflow with hope. By the power of the Holy Spirit. These words from the Bible distill a powerful truth. Hope characterises God's nature, and through the supernatural work of his Spirit, he empowers us to live in hope and impart it to others. In much of the worldwide church today, there is evidence of a rising tide of hope that is bringing new purpose and vigour to many.

Yet this is not universal. I also see many who have become disappointed, disillusioned, despairing, or even cynical about God, church, or their beliefs. Some have attempted to counter this with hype and religious formulae, cajoling themselves into positivism. However, hype is not real hope. Others live in passivity, grinding on in their walk with God, without the joy hope offers them.

Hope fuels the soul. It is one of the most powerful sustaining forces in life. You can take a person's freedom, finances, family or health, but he or she can endure the loss of these if hope remains. English clergyman and historian

Thomas Fuller once reflected, *"If it were not for hope, the heart would break."* [2]

Hope is waning in our secular, post-modern world. The moral erosion in society and violent global conditions are infecting many with one of the great diseases of our time: hopelessness. Hopelessness breeds passivity because it dulls the fire of passion in our souls. We may even be unaware of this sickness, but it shows up in the *"let's feast and get drunk, for tomorrow we die"*[3] attitude to life so prevalent today. The headlong rush for material possess-ions or the latest spiritual blessing only temporarily dulls the pain of diminished hope. Then we seek the next high. It is not more highs we need, but more hope – we need to become 'high on hope'.

Could these be the days Jesus warned of when he told the story of the five foolish bridesmaids?[4] They ran out of oil for their lamps when circumstances delayed the groom's arrival. Among other things, I believe the oil is the oil of joy, which flows from hope.[5] Was Jesus warning us that we would need overflowing hope to endure the troubled last days before he returned? I am certain he was.

Eventually, we all encounter painful situations where hope may be lost. However, the Lord promises, *"I will transform the valley of trouble into a gateway of hope."*[6] How strange yet wonderful that in times of great pain and difficulty God offers us an opportunity to gain an un-shakeable hope in him. In every valley, there is a doorway of hope waiting to be found. We can choose to be embittered or know him more intimately, to stay in the valley of despair or go through the gateway of hope. To find that gateway, it is essential that we understand the dynamics of hope, for, *"Everything that is done in the world,"* said the great German reformer Martin Luther, *"is done by hope."*[7]

At a time when dark spiritual forces are seeking to overwhelm many with fear and despair, God is offering a door of hope to a turbulent world that has found itself in a deep valley of trouble. And the church worldwide has the power to help the world find that door.

These past few decades, my wife's journey in battling Multiple Sclerosis, and my own through cancer and a heartbreaking church incident, has been one of hope; hope lost, and hope regained. This book is about that journey. In it, we will discover what true hope is, how it can be all too easily lost yet wonderfully regained, and how hardship, rather than being a killer of hope, can in fact be a potent ingredient in hope's development. We will consider the mystery of suffering, and try to make sense of what often appears to be beyond our understanding. Then we will look at the role work plays in promoting hope – many see no purpose in what they do and thus feel hopeless – and how the emerging church will be characterised by a worldview that sees all of life as its field of service. Finally, we will look at the ultimate reason for hope: the glorious future kingdom God has prepared for those who love him.

Wherever my wife and I have shared the things we have learned on our journey, we have seen God lift and inspire many by the message of hope. One woman summarised it best when she said, *"I have received permission to dream again."* It is my prayer that this book will similarly encourage you, and assist you to open a doorway of hope for others.

Notes
[1] Romans 15:13 (NIV)
[2] Thomas Fuller (1608 – 1661)
[3] 1 Corinthians 15: 32
[4] Matthew 25:1-13
[5] Hebrews 1:9
[6] Hosea 2:15
[7] Martin Luther (1483 – 1546)

TABLE OF CONTENTS

PART ONE

HOPE IN ADVERSITY

Hardship. Disappointment. Prolonged suffering. Why does God permit them and how do we maintain hope in the face of these all too common realities of life? The same circumstances may strike diverse people. While some become bitter and cynical, others grow in hope and sweetness of soul. What makes the difference?

This section provides some answers to these vexing questions, shows how hope can grow in even the most trying of circumstances and explains how to recover hope if it has been lost. Undeniably, hope that remains after suffering is true hope indeed.

Chapter One

Hope Is More Than Wishful Thinking

"Hope, like a gleaming taper's light,
Adorns and cheers our way;
And still, as darker grows the night,
Emits a brighter ray." [1]

The engine of the T-6 Texan trainer coughed, spluttered, and started to lose power. Alarmed, the pilot glanced at his instruments – the engine revolutions were dropping rapidly. Smoke began to pour from the exhaust. The hapless trainee radioed the problem to his flight commander who promptly ordered him to set his plane down on a country road below. As he and an accompanying trainee landed, a nearby work gang of coloured prison inmates, grateful for the reprieve from their tedious labour, looked up and watched the two aircraft land. When the pilots stepped out of their cockpits and removed their flying masks, the prisoners, and the white wardens, were stunned to see that they were black.

One of the prisoners, his eyes brightened and a smile beaming from his face, exclaimed, *"They're coloured flyers!"*

This scene is from the movie, *"The Tuskegee Airmen."* [2] Tuskegee was a United States Army Air Force training base in Alabama during World War II where black pilots were trained for combat. This was highly controversial in an America still racially divided, especially in the armed forces. Coloured soldiers usually received second line tasks and were not permitted to take part in combat missions. The training at Tuskegee was rigorous but many graduated and received their 'wings'. The majority went on to fly P-51 Mustang fighters in North Africa and Europe where they established an outstanding combat record. The white bomber squadrons, after initial prejudice, began to request the Tuskegee flyers to escort them on bombing raids, as it is claimed they never lost a single bomber they escorted, to enemy fighters.

What produced a smile on the face of the black prisoner? What caused such elation? *Hope.* The two black flyers gave him hope. He had seen something – that perhaps one day his country would treat blacks equally to whites – and that hope had lifted his soul. That is what hope does. It is one of the most powerful forces in the universe. In this chapter, I want to explain the true meaning of hope.

Definition of Hope

"I hope it doesn't rain."

"I hope I get the job."

"Hope you have a nice holiday."

Most of us use these or similar expressions everyday. Generally used to express wishful thinking, the word 'hope' has become diluted in its power. Biblical hope is very different. The entire Bible is a book of hope. Promises and stories of hope abound. Hope, in biblical terms, means a *'confident, joyful, and patient expectation of good.'*[3] Personal ambition or fantasy is not the basis for the good things we hope for; rather, God's promises and the desires he places within us form the foundation for genuine hope.

One commentator explains that biblical hope is not *"an optimistic outlook, or wishful thinking without any foundation, but confident expectation based on solid certainty."*[4] The prophet Jeremiah, speaking to Jewish captives in Babylon, said, *"'For I know the plans I have for you,' says the Lord. 'They are plans for good and not for disaster, to give you a future and a hope.'"*[5] Plans...to give you...hope. God's plans and promises for our lives underpin hope.

Hope is an anchor for our soul.[6] Shaky world conditions today are rocking many people, but in the midst of such turbulence, hope keeps us anchored to the peace of God. Hope doesn't see only what the world media reports, which is almost totally negative, but sees God's good plans. Hope is to do with the future, but inspires confidence in the present. This confidence produces patient endurance as we wait for what is promised. The apostle Paul put it like this: *"For in this hope we were saved. But hope that is seen is no hope at all. Who hopes for what he already has? But if we hope for what we do not have, we wait for it patiently."*[7]

'This hope' refers to the return of Jesus Christ to restore creation, and grant believers resurrection bodies, in which we will live forever and rule with Jesus over a new earth. *"Eternity is the divine treasure house,"* said renowned English actor and playwright William Mountford,[8] *"and hope is the window, by means of which mortals are permitted to see, as through a glass darkly, the things which God is preparing."*

While hope connects most strongly to the promise of Christ's return, God also gives hope for the current circumstances of our lives, because he cares for us. Often in prophetic ministry, the Holy Spirit will speak to people about everyday situations. He does it to create hope, for hope envisions a better future. Hope dreams of a better day and hope is the key to faith and love.

Faith, Hope and Love

The Bible says, *"There are three things that will endure – faith, hope, and love – and the greatest of these is love."* [9] Faith, hope and love last. Lives, marriages, businesses or churches built on these will remain long after those built on lesser things have collapsed. In our haste to give love the rightful prominence in this trio of foundational virtues, we may overlook the fact that hope generates both faith and love. Paul said, *"We have heard of your faith in Christ Jesus and of the love you have for all the saints – the faith and love that **spring from hope.**"* [10]

Hope fuels love, because hope keeps the soul sweet. A cynical soul embittered by the troubles and disappointments of life cannot love. A person full of hope will love God and will love others. *"Love lives on hope,"* said French tragedian Pierre Corneille, [11] *"and dies when hope is dead."* Equally, *"Love...hopes all things."* [12]

Hope is also the parent of faith. Or as one pastor put it, *"Faith grows in the soil of hope."* The Bible says simply, *"Faith is the confident assurance that what we hope for is going to happen."* [13] In other words:

- ❧ Hope is the Promised Land. Faith is the title deed to that land.

- ❧ Hope sees a possibility, a dream, a vision. Faith sees the fulfillment.

- ❧ Hope is future. Faith is present (it is as if you already have the thing you hope for.)

    Hope is the seed of promise. Faith gives wings to the promise.

    Hope is like a Christmas gift under a tree. Faith takes the gift and opens it.

Hope Soars

We can see an analogy to the relationship between faith, hope, and love in physics. The law of gravity says that objects will always fall to the earth. However, the law of aerodynamics, being a higher law, overcomes the law of gravity, and makes flight possible. It then takes a specially designed craft to make this happen.

Similarly, life has gravitational pull. We live in a fallen world. Things will happen in life to pull us down. Nevertheless, it is possible, through the hope that Christ gives us, to counteract this downward pull on our souls. Hope is like the law of aerodynamics, offering us the possibility of rising above life's pain, crises and difficulties. Faith is the aircraft that takes us there. Love is the fuel that propels the plane along. Isaiah the prophet said, *"Those who wait on (hope in) the Lord will find new strength. They will fly high on wings like eagles. They will run and not grow weary. They will walk and not faint."* [14]

Hope, then, is the central stem from which the branches of faith and love grow and bear fruit. Faith, hope and love always work best together. The apostle Paul said, *"We continually remember before our God and Father your **work produced by faith**, your **labour prompted by love**, and your **endurance inspired by hope** in our Lord Jesus Christ."* [15] Good work, service and endurance characterise lives founded on faith, hope and love.

In addition, faith, hope and love form powerful armour that will protect believers in the turbulent times of these last days. *"But let us who are of the day be sober,"* said Paul, *"putting on the breastplate of faith and love, and as a helmet the hope of salvation."* [16] What soldier in Iraq today would dare go on patrol without wearing body armour and a helmet? The risks of a terrorist bomb are just too great. Likewise, faith, hope and love form an impregnable shield that today's believers cannot afford to be without. This potent triplet can overcome the most desperate circumstances. It has powerfully helped my wife and me, and hope has become one of the defining themes of our life journey. In the next chapters, let me share some of our story....

Notes

[1] Oliver Goldsmith, Irish author and poet (1728-1774).

[2] *The Tuskegee Airmen,* © HBO movies, 1995.

[3] In the Old Testament, there are various Hebrew words used for hope, but two occur most frequently. One is the word *tiqvah* (Strong's H8615). Figuratively this means *hope, expectation, something yearned for and anticipated eagerly.* Literally, it means *a rope or cord of attachment.* The other is *yachel* (Strong's H3716). This means *to be patient, to wait, to hope.* In the New Testament, one Greek word is mainly used. It is the word *elpis* (Strong's G1680), which has the meaning *expectation, confidence, anticipation.*

[4] *Spirit Filled Life Bible,* Nashville, Thomas Nelson Publishers, 1991; see 'word wealth,' p. 1826, referring to the Greek term elpis.

[5] Jeremiah 29:11

[6] Hebrews 6:19a (NIV)

[7] Romans 8:24,25 (NIV)

[8] William Mountford (1664 – 1692)

[9] 1 Corinthians 13:13

[10] Colossians 1:4,5a (NIV)

[11] Pierre Corneille (1606-1684)

[12] 1 Corinthians 13:7 (RSV)

[13] Hebrews 11:1

[14] Isaiah 40:31

[15] 1 Thessalonians 1:3 (NIV)
[16] 1 Thessalonians 5:8 (NKJV)

Chapter Two

Hope Will Get You Through

"Faith walks simply, childlike,
Between the darkness of human life
And the hope of what is to come." [1]

At twenty, Lynn Pengelly was young and attractive, but she was dying. She wanted to be a nurse, to help sick people regain their health, and had eagerly commenced her training, but a year later a routine X-ray cruelly revealed a growth on her lung. The doctors did their best, but could not contain the cancer. *"Your daughter has only a few months to live,"* they told her father and mother. Deciding that the best place for Lynn was with them, her parents brought her home.

She accepted her fate and didn't complain. Her courage and peace as death approached touched the frequent visitors who came to see her. But as the weeks dragged on, the pain became unbearable and every breath a struggle. Finally she asked her father, *"Why doesn't Jesus come for me?"* He studied her face, still beautiful despite the wasting disease. No father should have to answer such a question, he thought. *"He will come when he is ready, sweetheart."*

A few hours later, Lynn died. However, hers was no lone journey to heaven. She must have seen him, for her face reflected his splendour and shone with a serenity that not even death could erase. Those who came into the room where she lay wept when they saw it. Beauty accompanied her passing.

That evening her grieving mother turned to the Bible for comfort. It had been her daily practice to read it to her daughter. The scheduled text for that day was from the Song of Solomon. The words, clearly meant for Lynn, said:

"Arise, my darling, my beautiful one,

And come with me.

See! The winter is past;

The rains are over and gone.

Flowers appear on the earth;

The season of singing has come." [2]

I first heard this story from Lynn's younger sister Jane. It was early 1976. She and her mother had travelled from England to visit relatives in New Zealand. One Sunday, Jane spoke at the church I attended in my hometown of Blenheim, a large, rural township situated near the top of the beautiful South Island, one of New Zealand's two main islands. She explained how Lynn's death, far from being tragic, had powerfully drawn her and many others to God. The congregation was hushed as she vividly described Lynn's last moments. Some wept; all were moved. However, it was not only the story that drew my attention. Tall, slender, and bronzed by the continual sunny days the region enjoyed, Jane looked lovely. *"That's exactly the sort of woman I would love to marry,"* I thought to myself. I discovered later that she had noticed me from the front of the church and asked who I was. Soon after, a mutual friend arranged for us to have a meal together. As we conversed over dinner, this gorgeous brunette with the deep brown eyes stole my heart.

During the rest of that summer, we frequently climbed the hill behind the farm cottage Jane stayed at on the outskirts of town. From the top, we surveyed the scene before us: emerald pastures speckled with sheep, fields golden with wheat and sunsets that painted the sky dazzling red. In that pleasant setting, we talked for hours.

I discovered that a few years after Lynn's death, her father had died suddenly, probably of a broken heart, and not long after, Jane herself had been diagnosed with a serious illness. She had attempted to walk down the stairs at her home one morning, curiously missed some steps, and fell to the base of the stairway. She was whisked to the doctor, who promptly ordered medical tests in the hospital. The eventual diagnosis was Multiple Sclerosis (MS), a degenerative disease of the central nervous system. Having recovered from that first attack, Jane was in remission when we met.

Marriage

Soon we had fallen completely in love, but MS threatened us. *"Do you realise what this disease could do?"* well meaning friends and family pointed out. *"Jane could be confined to a wheelchair unable to do anything for herself."* We hoped their predictions wouldn't come true. Anyway, how could I walk away from the woman I had fallen hopelessly in love with? We would have to trust God with our future. A year later, we married. As I watched my radiant bride walk down the aisle, I marvelled at God's goodness in bringing us together from opposite sides of the world.

Holding hands, we took our vows, and didn't realise then how severely tested they would be.

Our doctor advised that having children could aggravate my wife's condition, but we wanted to be parents. Her health had been good, except for awful migraines that occurred every few months. Forced to lie in a darkened room, she suffered nausea and severe pain, unable to eat anything. This would last for two to three days and had been a pattern since the age of three.

Within a few months, Jane was pregnant with our first child. The migraines, however, did not cease, and this began to provoke me. One day, in the middle of a new bout, I could not bear to see my wife suffer any longer. I began to see this as one of those circumstances in life that are like storms. They blow into our lives and incapacitate us physically, emotionally or spiritually. We seek shelter from some storms by hiding in and trusting God, we endure others through faith and patience, but I felt this was one to resist. Therefore, I refused to accept it – in fact, I became very angry.

My wife lay ill in the bedroom, while I prayed in an adjacent room. Jesus sometimes healed the sick by rebuking the evil spirit behind the illness, so, calling on the name of Jesus, I commanded the spirit causing the migraine to go and asked God to set my wife free. Not every migraine is demonic in origin, but I believed this one was. After I prayed for a while, I asked Jane how she was. No change. I repeated this pattern four or five times. Still no change. Once more I prayed; once more I asked how she felt. *"The pain is gone!"* she replied. The pain and nausea had left instantly, and she has never had another migraine since. The Lord completely healed her. I sometimes wonder what would have happened if I had given up too soon. Strangely, the same approach with MS didn't yield a similar result – it would prove to be a storm to endure.

After this, Jane enjoyed a trouble free pregnancy until the sixth month, when she spiked high temperatures from an infection. Antibiotics were prescribed to treat it, but she suffered an allergic reaction, which, with the fever, brought on premature labour. Our son, Joseph, weighed just under one and a quarter kilograms (two pounds eleven ounces) at birth. Because his tiny lungs were underdeveloped, the medical staff gave him a fifty-fifty chance of survival in the first three days. Day by day, we stood by his incubator and watched his little chest heave in and out, as he struggled for breath. We, and others, prayed fervently for him during that time. He survived and six weeks later, we took him home. Today he is healthy, married to Katherine, and has children of his own.

Pastoral Ministry

By early 1978, we had moved to Picton, a picturesque seaside town about twenty minutes drive north of Blenheim, to lead a newly planted church. After two years, I resigned from my teaching position at a Blenheim high school, in order to pastor the growing church fulltime. By then our second son, Adam, had been born. It was after this that Jane experienced more frequent relapses of MS. One particularly bad attack robbed her of the use of her hands. *"How bad would things get? How would we cope with the demands of pastoral ministry?"* I wondered. We felt both frustrated and scared. Although we believed God healed the sick, we needed a specific answer from him.

One day, I shut myself in my office, lay on the floor and cried to the Lord, *"How long do we have to endure this? You heal the sick, but will you heal my wife? Where are your compassion and mercy?"* An answer soon came. The next day, as I read the Bible, the following verse caught my attention: *"As you know, we consider blessed those who have*

31

persevered. You have heard of Job's perseverance and have seen what the Lord finally brought about. The Lord is full of compassion and mercy." [3]

God had answered each of my questions in the order I had asked them – all from one verse. Yes, we would need to endure; yes, there would be a positive outcome (Job was healed); yes, the Lord was compassionate and merciful! Comforted, we felt like the psalmist who said, *"Remember your word to your servant, for you have given me hope. My comfort in suffering is this: your promise preserves my life."* [4]

God had spoken so clearly to us (we thought then that clarity meant speed, not realising that the more clearly God speaks, the longer the fulfillment often takes, as he shapes our lives to handle what has been promised). About this time, other people had dreams and prophetic words concerning Jane being healed. Faith grew within us.

During the next few years, we moved north to Wellington, New Zealand's capital city, to lead a church that traced its origins back to revival meetings held by English evangelist Smith Wigglesworth in the 1920's. By now it was small and struggling, a shadow of its former glory. People, even other pastors, weren't very encouraging; I was told that the city was dark, a preacher's graveyard, and that few people ever came to Christ! That provoked me. I prayed. I fasted. I said, *"Lord, give me souls, or I die!"* I had read about a missionary praying that prayer and figured if it worked for him, it might work for me. I'm glad God didn't take me literally, but at least he knew I was eager. I visualised people getting saved every week; and they did.

In fact, at our farewell service in Picton, a lady received Christ and then said, *"I will see you next week in Wellington."* She lived there and had been visiting Picton for the weekend! Sure enough, the following week, she was at the church with her family, and a number of them also received

Christ. From that very first Sunday in Wellington, people were saved weekly.

There, our third son, Tim, was born, and the MS symptoms that had previously been temporary became permanent and more severe, so that by 1985 Jane was able to walk only very short distances and needed a wheelchair. This dreadful disease was swallowing up my lovely, vivacious wife and I felt I was losing her.

Jane's mum, affectionately known as 'Jeannie,' came to live with us around that time. If it had not been for her commitment to help us over the years, I am not sure how we would have coped. She is a true hero. Although today she no longer lives with us, she displays, for someone in her eighties, a hunger for God that is an inspiration to us all.

My wife received prayer for healing many times, but with no improvement, and this attracted much advice.

"Have more faith."

"Don't admit Jane is sick; confess she is healed already and healing will come."

"Don't look at the circumstances – look to God."

However, none of these told us how faith and hope really worked. Were we to ignore the very real pain of our situation? Someone once said:

"God calls the things that are not, as if they were; but he does not call the things that are, as if they were not."

To believe the word of God, we do not need to deny the reality of our present circumstances. Abraham, the father of faith, is our example in this. The apostle Paul said, *"Abraham is the father of all who believe...Abraham believed in the God who brings the dead back to life and who brings into existence what didn't exist before (calls things that are not as though they were)."* [5]

Yet Abraham did not pretend his present reality was nonexistent. *"Without weakening in his faith he faced the fact that his body was as good as dead – since he was about a hundred years old – and that Sarah's womb was dead."* 6 He faced the facts. *"Faith does not deny the facts,"* said one evangelist, *"it changes the facts."*

We could not deny that Jane's condition was worsening. However we had a powerful promise from God. She had been healed from migraines – surely MS was no harder to heal? *"In all things,"* said the German philosopher Goethe, *"it is better to hope than to despair."* 7 We chose to hope – this helped us to get through that time. Little did we know that things were about to get much worse.

Notes
1 Catherine de Hueck Doherty, Catholic author and scholar (1896-1985)
2 Song of Solomon 2:10, 11 (NIV)
3 James 5:11 (NIV)
4 Psalm 119:49, 50 (NIV)
5 Romans 4:16, 17 (Part in brackets is NIV)
6 Romans 4:19 (NIV)
7 Johann Wolfgang von Goethe (1749-1832)

Chapter Three

A Double Blow

*"Faith laughs at that which
Fear weeps over."* [1]

I had felt unwell all year. It was 1985, the same year Jane started to use a wheelchair. The church we led in Wellington had grown, with people continuing to come to faith in Christ. I was juggling the demands of pastoral ministry, helping my wife and trying, rather unsuccessfully, to give my children time and attention. The truth was that by the time 1985 arrived, and after three years in the city, I was stressed by all the pressure.

That year I developed chest pains that became particularly acute after eating. My doctor thought it was indi-gestion, but the prescribed medicine did nothing to alleviate the symptoms. I dragged myself from one thing to another, and put the constant tiredness down to being too busy. I began to shrink from new demands and became quite negative. People who knew me said I was different – it was as if the light in me had gone out. It was scary as I didn't know what was happening to me. Was this spiritual opposition, burn out or something more sinister?

Towards the end of the year, I discovered a sizeable lump in my groin. It seemed to appear suddenly, as I had not noticed it before. Shrugging it off, I hoped that it would somehow go away. It was just one more thing I did not need to think about. Jane, however, having been a cardiac technician, was more medically aware and insisted that I see the doctor immediately. So I made the reluctant trek to his office. He said it might be cancer. Cancer. Now that is a chilling word. It dawned on me that I might be about to face a bigger battle than I thought.

My doctor ordered a biopsy, but as it was a few weeks before Christmas, it would be the New Year before I could have it. Those weeks of waiting should have been tense with anxiety; instead a glorious peace descended on me. *"Come to me all of you who are weary and carry heavy burdens, and I will give you rest,"* Jesus promised, *"Take my yoke upon you. Let me teach you, because I am humble and gentle, and you will find rest for your souls."* [2] I began to see myself connected to Jesus, with him bearing the load of my situation. An intimacy with him developed that I had not known before, and with it came that wonderful peace.

Early in the New Year of 1986, I went to hospital for my biopsy. As I waited nervously in the ward for the procedure to take place, I opened the Bible, turned to the reading for that day, and read, *"Blessed is he who has regard for the weak; the Lord delivers him in times of trouble. The Lord will protect him and preserve his life…the Lord will sustain him on his sickbed and restore him from his bed of illness."* [3] How incredible that of all the words in the Bible, these were the ones I read that day.

At home, Jane agonised over the situation. She cried out to God, *"Are you going to take him from me? What will happen to the children and me?"* She also turned to the Bible for comfort. As we both used the same reading guide, she came to the identical verses. Reading them filled her with peace, and she knew everything would be all right. Two other friends also contacted us with exactly the same scriptures and felt they were applicable to us.

A short time later, the doctor gave us the news. I had Hodgkin's disease, a type of cancer of the lymphatic system. It had infected my chest, neck, and groin. There was an eighty percent chance of recovery with chemotherapy, and treatment was to commence in a few weeks. In the space of a year, I had seen Multiple Sclerosis confine my wife to a wheelchair and I had developed cancer. This was a huge double blow.

I was to have nine rounds of chemotherapy. Each round would be monthly, with two weeks on drugs, and two off. The first few cycles produced some nausea, and an agitated mental state caused by a steroid that was part of the cocktail of drugs I took. Some were taken orally, and the major drug by injection. Inflamed, the injected vein radiated a fierce pain into the rest of my arm. Later, the drug was given diluted in an intravenous drip which helped alleviate this.

After my second round, the leading church of our movement flew my wife and me to Auckland, New Zealand's largest city, to pray for us in a healing service they were conducting. In discomfort from a fresh injection, I felt the pain in my arm completely disappear after prayer. When we returned to Wellington, a new scan revealed no cancer nodules in my body. My oncologist was pleased but recommended that I complete the course of chemotherapy – another seven months – in order to destroy any cancer cells the scan could not detect. I agreed to this. Some may argue with my decision to continue treatment, but I did not see submitting to my doctor's advice as contradicting faith in God.

In fact, people ask if it was prayer or drugs that healed me. I think it was both. We and others certainly prayed. Everyday, Jane and I declared defeat to every trace of cancer in my body. God is both miracle healer and creator of medicinal substances. Ask Israel's King Hezekiah – he was healed from a terminal disease through a poultice made from figs, after he prayed to the Lord. [4] God responded, *"I have heard your prayer ...and will heal you."* God heals by miracles *and* medicine.

The decision to continue chemotherapy would be bitter sweet, however. During the following months I became very ill. Severe nausea and inability to concentrate were common most days, and sleeplessness many nights. I also obsessed over little things. One time, with hammer and nails in hand, I intended to nail down a floor mat that moved irritatingly out of position when someone walked over it. My wife and mother-in-law intersected me before I could do it. That mat bothered me for months. Half way through the treatment, with a suppressed immune system, I developed pneumonia. I longed for the two weeks each month free of drugs, and dreaded each new round.

People were very kind to us during this time. One family started to pray with me at the commencement of every round, the side effects becoming less severe. Two pastors from other churches gave us generous gifts of finance. Another church took an offering for us. Our own church put a new roof on our house, with a family financing it. This kindness touched our family deeply – God softened the pain of that year through the love of others.

Our three boys, Joseph, Adam and Tim were aged eight, six and two at this time. People in the church were wonderful, inviting them to stay, transporting them to school and taking them for treats. It must not have been easy for them to see their parents' flagging health. Today, they all have a greater sensitivity to, and compassion for, the needs of others, which I think stems from what they have seen.

Finally, after nine months, chemotherapy ended. The doctors pronounced me in remission. That is their word. In fact, I have been healed of the disease ever since, because on a hospital bed one morning, God promised to *'restore me from my bed of illness.'* If it had not been for the hope he had given us, the faith that grew from that hope, and the love and support of many friends, we would have been overwhelmed.

Yet the battle was not quite over. The cancer treatment had one last sting in its tail. The same church that had flown us to their healing service suggested we take a three month break in Auckland to recover. It had been a hard year – the hardest of our lives – and some time out would help us recuperate. Looking forward to the rest, I imagined returning home to continue leading the church in full health.

A few weeks before leaving, a rash appeared on my chest and the left side of my face. It burned and grew increasingly painful. Soon it erupted into watery blisters. My doctor said it was the worst case of shingles he had ever seen and that there was no treatment. I was glad he was impressed. Apparently, the chemotherapy had so depleted my immune system that a virus had attacked part of my nervous system, causing the shingles. On obtaining a second opinion from my oncologist, I was sent to the hospital and treated with a newly developed antiviral drug. Soon the blisters subsided, but the damage to the nerves left me with pain so excruciating that I received morphine. It was about this time that I started to identify closely with Job and his painful boils!

We finally arrived in Auckland, and found that the church there had rented a house, stocked it with food, paid the rent and utilities for the duration of our stay, arranged for schooling for the children and assigned a family to help us any way they could. We felt such incredible love and care from people at that time. The post-shingles pain continued unabated however and six weeks into the break, I was still in agony. Everything in me screamed out, *"Why? Why was this happening to me?"* Then I remembered something I once heard another pastor say: *"In difficult times, do not ask why, but who?"* In other words, don't ask why is this happening to me but who am I becoming through this?

So I began to ask what God was trying to teach me. The realisation dawned that I would be unfit to return to my church in Wellington. One Sunday, Jane and I made the difficult decision to resign from the pastorate of my church and move to Auckland for a time of recuperation. That night at a church service, God healed me. I had been prayed for many times before with no result, but that night during a healing time, the pain completely left me. It was as if God had waited for me to come to the decision to resign. I had been so determined to return and lead my church that God had had to get my attention. He now had it.

So we moved north to Auckland to begin a new chapter in our lives. After a welcome year off, I joined the staff of our church there. Looking back now, I realise that God's grace and a sense of his nearness saw us through that very dark time. His promise to us had produced peace and an unshakable hope in his goodness that helped us endure. Hope, we discovered, is one of the most powerful sustaining forces in the world. And if it is lost, our world begins to collapse, as we shall discover in the next chapter.

Notes

[1] Charles Spurgeon, famed English preacher and author (1834 - 1892).

[2] Matthew 11:28,29

[3] Psalm 41:1-3 (NIV)

[4] 2 Kings 20:1-7

Chapter Four

Watch Out for the Hopekillers

"My days are over.
My hopes have disappeared.
My heart's desires are broken." [1]

One sunny August day in 1998, a phone call changed my life. Twelve years had passed since my battle with cancer and Jane's confinement to a wheelchair. By the end of 1990, Jane had lost the ability to stand or hold anything with her hands. Therefore, I had resigned from the staff of our church in order to care for her and the children fulltime. Although it was difficult, I still managed to serve on the eldership team.

Frustration crept into my new role as caregiver. Naturally unsuited to being a nurse, hairdresser, make-up artist and a host of other roles, I longed to escape back to 'full time ministry'! Then I recalled Jesus said that whatever we do to even one of the least of his brethren, we do to him. [2] Gradually I appreciated that care of Jane and the children was as valid and important a ministry as any I had ever done. Today I am dangerously good with lipstick and mascara! Grace for the caregiver role settled on me and, although there were times of weariness and difficulty, Jane and I remained full of hope for the future. All this was about to change.

We had returned to my hometown of Blenheim for a family celebration. On the day of the event, the phone rang at the house where we were staying. It was the assistant pastor of our church in Auckland. After we exchanged pleasantries, his voice grew solemn.

"You have to come home straightaway," he stated. Now this pastor was known for his practical jokes on unsuspecting victims, and I concluded he was at it again. So I told him to stop joking.

"No, I'm serious," he insisted. *"You have to come back to Auckland as soon as you can."*

"Why? What's happened?"

"The elders have discovered that the senior pastor has had an affair with one of the women in the church. We have confronted him about it, and he has confessed."

I could not believe it. This man had been a friend to Jane and me, a leader we respected, and a father figure to us and many others. That evening, with heavy hearts, we attended the family function. The next day we caught an early flight and flew home.

So began a heartbreaking saga of betrayal, broken relationships and grief. The elders discovered that the pastor had been involved with more than one woman, which added to the pain we felt. The church, at that time one of the largest in the country, lost two-thirds of the congregation in just a few years. I watched hundreds of disappointed people lose hope, some of whom have not yet recovered. I had maintained hope in Jane's and my battle with sickness, but now a dark cloud of hopelessness descended on me. Confusion, anger, depression and a growing cynicism took hold, and I seemed powerless to stop it.

"It is the fog of disillusionment," the Lord replied [3] when I asked Him about it. *"The only way through is by revelation."* So I prayed for revelation. In the next few years, I learned much about making sense of suffering, and about hope. I learned that bitterness leads to cynicism, but forgiveness leads to renewed hope; that there are things that restore hope, and things that kill hope, giving rise to one of the great diseases of the modern age: hopelessness.

The Disease of Hopelessness

Like any disease, the disease of hopelessness has symptoms. These may include the following:

- Loss of joy and growing depression. There may even be suicidal thoughts – these may be strong or fleeting, but show that there is little hope for the future.

- Emotional numbness – it is hard to get excited about anything, and difficult to love others or respond to their love.

- Low self-worth – when hope is gone, our cause for living is lost. With no cause, our lives become devalued and without meaning. This leads to low self-worth.

- Unbelief – it is not easy to trust God and other people. Faith erodes when hope is dying. This can lead to cynicism and scepticism.

- ✌ Spiritual passivity – instead of passion there is lethargy and dullness. Worship, prayer and other Christian disciplines become a struggle.

- ✌ Addictions – food, television, drugs, illicit sexual behaviour and so on, may be increasingly turned to, bringing a temporary, but false, comfort.

These are just a few. If two, three, or more of these symptoms are present in our lives, then hope is dying. A number of factors can cause this.

Disappointment

The book of Proverbs says, *"Hope deferred makes the heart sick."* [4] The continued postponement of things we have hoped for, prayed about and believed for, is disappointing. Orison Marden [5], founder of the modern success movement, said, *"There is no medicine like hope, no incentive so great, and no tonic so powerful as expectation of something better tomorrow."* When expectation ceases because tomorrow never arrives, the heart becomes sick.

Waiting for the invisible to become manifest is dangerous business. Missionary statesman J. Oswald Sanders talked about the 'slowness of God.' *"The apparent slowness of God to act when to us action seems urgent and imperative unless all is to be lost,"* he writes, *"can be a great challenge to our faith."* [6] This apparent slowness, when we are convinced the thing hoped for should come quickly, will indeed test us. When answers to prayer seem delayed and hopes remain unfulfilled, or when people, especially leaders, have let us down, we may misinterpret this as God letting us down. In reality, he is working out his higher plan in our lives – he is perfectly good and always perfectly on time.

Disillusionment

"Where there is no vision," wrote King Solomon, *"the people perish."* [7] Job, that great example of inexplicable suffering, put it this way: *"But I do not have the strength to endure. I do not have a goal that encourages me to carry on."* [8] Hope sees. Hope dreams. When the dream or vision becomes dimmed, hope will die. We become disappointed. Disappointment turns to disillusionment. We question whether the dream or prophecy was ever right in the first place. Tired of waiting, we become disillusioned and let the dream go.

In my season of disappointment, I began to doubt everything I had ever heard: the dream of Jane enjoying good health, dreams of serving God, promises for the church and nation. Were they wrong? Had I heard incorrectly? As I look back now, I realise that I was over-reacting, but at the time, it was very real.

My pastor's fall also opened my eyes to the perils of inauthentic Christian living. So many people lose their faith because of the gap between what is professed and what is done. If what we do on a Monday does not match up with what we do on a Sunday, it is inauthentic. We have to be the same; that is called integrity. Integrity means we are the same in the meeting as we are at home; we are as zealous to do a good day's work as we are to lift our hands and worship God. Every sphere of life is important to God, not only congregational or devotional spheres.

In a great deal of the Western church, we have heard much and often done little. The West idolises knowledge, but Jesus said the person who hears his words and does not act on them is like the person who built his house on sand.[9] God warned Israel before they entered Canaan, *"If you refuse to listen to the Lord your God and do not obey all the commands and laws I am giving you today ...the Lord himself will send against you...confusion and disillusionment in everything you do."* [10]

As I became disillusioned, I hungered for a Christianity that was real and authentic in all of life. In the big things and the little things. In the pursuit of miracles as well as small acts of kindness. In the congregation and in the workplace.

Now, authenticity and perfection are not the same. Authentic Christians, though desiring perfection, do not presume to be perfect. They admit their weaknesses and confess their faults, even to watching family, friends and workmates. It is called being real. The apostle Paul said, *"I don't mean to say that I have already...reached perfection! But I keep working toward that day when I will finally be all that Christ Jesus saved me for and wants me to be."* [11] Perfection is a lifetime journey.

What we see in others may dishearten us. If we look hard enough we will always find fault. We can be disillusioned by that or let it provoke us to become individuals of integrity and authenticity in our Christian walk. The choice is ours.

Despair

Speaking of a time when he endured intense persecution, the apostle Paul wrote, *"We do not want you to be uninformed, brothers, about the hardships we endured in the province of Asia. We were under pressure far beyond our ability to endure, so that we despaired of life. Indeed, in our heart we felt the sentence of death."* [12]

It is often taught that God will not test us beyond our ability to endure. This is based on the scripture that says, *"No temptation has seized you except what is common to man. And God is faithful; he will not let you be tempted beyond what you can bear. But when you are tempted, he will also provide a way out so that you can stand up under it."* [13]

True, God will never let us be tempted to sin beyond our ability to endure. However, this is not the same for trials that test our character. At times, we may face prolonged or intense suffering and hardship beyond our ability to endure. Job spoke of this. *"I, too, have been assigned months of futility, long and weary nights of misery. When I go to bed, I think, 'When will it be morning?' But the night drags on, and I toss till dawn."* [14] Job's suffering was so intense he wished he was dead. *"Why didn't you let me die at birth?"* he protested to God, *"then I would have been spared this miserable existence."* [15] Paul, too, felt he was under the sentence of death.

Despair is a serious state to descend into. It is the complete loss or absence of hope. Despairing people often long for death. It is Satan's attempt to abort what God is attempting to create in their lives for good. God restored Job and delivered Paul, and will do the same for us, if we do not lose heart.

Idealism

Idealism kills hope. It always looks for a better future – a more perfect day ahead – and it derides the present. When, in an imperfect world, things often do not work out, the idealist becomes easily disappointed. Hope is different. Hope looks for a better future as well, but sees the present as a stepping-stone towards that future. Although it feels the same dissatisfaction with the present as idealism, hope embraces current difficulties and sufferings as the pathway towards God's purposes and dreams.

For example, many Christians rightly long for a restored church – a church more like early Christianity. But we can idealise this. We hold up the ideal image of what the church should look like and compare it with the present. In doing so, many have turned away from the church, frustrated with the way it is. While this may be valid for those God leads to pioneer new expressions of being the church, others end up in a wilderness, without a Christian community to relate to.

People of hope, however, while gripped with the promise of a revived and restored church, embrace the present, imperfect as it is, and work to move the church forward. They appreciate that churches comes in all shapes and sizes, forms and structures, but if the heart is right, God loves them all. They love what God loves. I love my wife no less because she is in a wheelchair. Although I long to see her free and restored, that does not diminish the love I feel for her. So it is with God. He sees the church that will be, but by his grace loves the church that is. And so should we. He is working to restore all things, and one day everything will be perfect.

Demons

Certain types of evil spirits especially kill hope. Some of these are spirits of unbelief, fear, depression, discouragement, death or hopelessness. At times of vulnerability, they may attack us, generating negative thoughts and feelings that are beyond the ordinary. Anyone who is prophetic will be particularly prone to attack. The prophetic gift and ministry is to encourage others and inspire hope. Therefore, the devil will target it because he is the arch discourager.

For example, a spirit of discouragement can sweep ordinary discouragement into such intensity that we find it hard to function. Normal discouragement is overcome by faith in God's word. Demonic discouragement needs faith and deliverance. A spirit of death may not cause actual death, but rather seek to kill the prophetic dream we carry. It will try to bring death to the gift and call of God on our lives, pushing us to give up through intense discouragement. We need to resist such spirits. If we submit to God and resist them, they will flee. If they do not, then we need the prayers of others. Sometimes we may be unaware we are under such attack, and only conscious that something is terribly wrong.

As I struggled to cope with the fall of the pastor of my church, I became depressed. Joy fled, I could not function and my thoughts were continually negative. This probably was a result of grief from the loss of a spiritual father and leader, nevertheless, I felt strongly enough to mention it to my fellow elders. God-permitted disillusionment was one thing; intense depression was another. As they prayed for me, they discerned a depressive spirit hovering around me like a dark cloud. They rebuked it and commanded it to go. Immediately I felt as if a heavy weight lifted off me. I still had to work through the feelings of grief and disappointment in the months to come, but that moment was a turning point.

There is Hope

The Bible says, *"If a tree is cut down, there is hope that it will sprout again and grow new branches. Though its roots have grown old in the earth and its stump decays, at the scent of water it may bud and sprout again like a new seedling."* [16] We will sometimes feel that there is nothing more than a stump of our dreams left. Take heart that hope can be recovered. Consider the words of a popular song:

"When I am down and, oh my soul, so weary,

When troubles come and my heart burdened be;

Then, I am still and wait here in the silence,

Until you come and sit awhile with me

You raise me up, so I can stand on mountains,

You raise me up, to walk on stormy seas;

I am strong, when I am on your shoulder

You raise me up ... To more than I can be." [17]

'I am strong when I am on your shoulder.' This is like a little girl at a parade. The band leads the way, and one by one, the colourful floats glide by, but the child is at the back of the crowd. She cannot see anything through the forest of legs. What does she do? She turns to her father and lifts her arms upwards – the universal signal for, *"Pick me up."* Her father bends down, scoops up the child, and places her onto his shoulders. From that vantage point, the excited little girl now sees the parade.

At times, we may lose sight of the parade of life because the things that kill hope have crowded out the view. Once we were at the front cheering the parade on. Gradually, we have slipped to the back of the crowd and can no longer see clearly. But the Father waits. He waits for the universal sign. It may take us months or even years, but if we lift our hands and hearts to him, he will bend down, pick us up, and hoist us onto his shoulders. *"Let the beloved of the Lord rest secure in him,"* says the Bible, *"for he shields him all day long, and the one the Lord loves rests between his shoulders."* [18] We are strong when we are on his shoulders. From there we see again. Hope is restored. Light and rest come again to our souls. God is the great restorer of hope.

Notes

1 Job 17:11

2 Matthew 25:40 (NKJV)

3 Some may ask whether God speaks like this today, given that the Bible is the greatest source of revelation from him. There are however, many circumstances in life that the Bible does not speak

directly to. Hence, God may speak through visions, dreams, impressions, thoughts, other people, and prophecy. As long as these do not violate scripture they are valid. The New Testament is full of examples of God speaking in these ways to many people, and his Spirit still does so today.

For an excellent discussion on the fact that God still speaks to his children today, see *Surprised by the Voice of God* by Jack Deere, Eastbourne, Kingsway Publications, 1996.

4 Proverbs 13:12a (RSV)

5 Orison Marden (1850-1924)

6 J. Oswald Sanders, *Spiritual Problems,* Eastbourne, Victory Press, 1972, p.28.

7 Proverbs 29:18 (KJV)

8 Job 6:11

9 Matthew 7:26

10 Deuteronomy 28:15,20

11 Philippians 3: 12

12 2 Corinthians 1:8-9a (NIV)

13 1 Corinthians 10:13 (NIV)

14 Job 7:3,4

15 Job 10:18b,19a

16 Job 14:7-9

17 *You Raise Me Up* by Secret Garden, from the album *Once in a Red Moon,* © Universal Music Publishing, Norway and Acorn Music, Ireland, 2002.

18 Deuteronomy 33:12 (NIV)

Chapter Five

Restored Hope and Chocolate

"Hope is the power of being cheerful,
In circumstances which we know to be desperate." [1]

It was early 1977 and Jane and I had been married for a month. It was a long, warm summer, so one afternoon, we headed to the beach with some friends. After a refreshing swim, I lay down in the sun, and soon dozed off. I then had the most vivid dream.

I saw a street paved with cobbled stones. Houses, joined together and lining either side of the street, stretched into the distance. It reminded me of an old English town. As Jane and I walked along the street, a third person – I could tell it was Jesus – walked with us. We stopped at the houses and knocked on the doors. While some of the occupants refused to let us in or even open their doors, others welcomed us and invited us inside. We talked with them about the Lord and explained the Gospel to them. We continued to do this all the way down the street. Then the dream ended abruptly.

At that point, I woke up and wondered what it all meant. As I prayed for understanding, the Holy Spirit said to me, *"The street is the world and the houses are nations. Some will be open to you and some will not."* Could it be that God was calling Jane and me to travel and minister in various nations? The thought of an international ministry swelled me with self-importance. However, the Lord has had millennia of experience at killing ambition and pride in his servants. As the years rolled by, and Jane's health deteriorated and confined her to a wheelchair, I assumed the dream must have been just my imagination, and forgot about it. Then something strange happened.

Twenty-five years after I first had it, and towards the end of my intense season of disillusionment, the dream started to come back to me. I tried to dismiss it, but it would not go away. In fact, it taunted me. How impossible, I thought to myself. *"Hope deferred makes the heart sick,"* says the proverb,[2] and that's exactly how I felt.

Finally, I prayed, *"Lord that's how I feel – heartsick. Jane hasn't been healed, we're more confined than ever, and this dream won't go away!"* Then, the Lord drew my attention to the second part of that proverb. *"But desire fulfilled is a tree of life."* He said to me, *"David, I am changing the season over yours and others' lives. There has been a season of deferred hope among many of my people and they have become disillusioned. But I am changing the season to one of desires fulfilled."*

Hope rose within me. Could the dream be real after all? *"Well Lord, heal Jane and we'll go,"* I responded. *"David how long are you going to sit around?"* the Lord countered, *"Don't wait for healing, just move."* Solomon once wrote, *"If you wait for perfect conditions, you'll never get anything done."*[3] It never pays to argue with God, as he will not listen to our excuses.

The point of impossibility, despair, and dead ambition is the point when the dream can live. I would have rather gone with Jane walking by my side, but we had to obey. Around this time, a number of people said to us that we should travel and minister within the nation. But how could we do this practically?

Some time later, a car salesman contacted me to discuss a specialized vehicle that he thought might interest me. It was a modified people mover. A disabled person could sit in a wheelchair in the front passenger position, next to the driver. An automatic ramp on the passenger's side allowed for easy access in and out of the cabin. Due to the vehicle being modified overseas, the price was unaffordable, but it opened our eyes to the possibility of easier travel. Later, we discovered a New Zealand company who was modifying a similar vehicle to do the same job. The price was about half that of the first vehicle. We decided to go ahead and take a loan on our house. I struggled with the thought of increasing our mortgage, but if this vehicle would help us fulfill the dream, the price was worth it.

We also applied to a government agency for a grant. They told us that due to a previous grant, we would be eligible to apply in six months and, if approved, could receive up to twenty-two thousand dollars, over a quarter of the price of the vehicle. They pointed out however, that there was huge pressure on funds, and they were only meeting a third of requests. Feeling strongly that it had to be sooner and surer than this, we prayed and asked the Lord to supply the same amount.

We ordered a vehicle and booked the modification. Finance began to come in. Friends gave us six thousand dollars. A Christian businessman, paralyzed in an accident, sent us another ten thousand. We received three thousand dollars discount on the purchase of the vehicle and a further three thousand discount on the modifications. Twenty-two thousand dollars – the exact amount of the government grant.

The day finally came to collect the vehicle from the factory. To take Jane for a drive in it was a thrill. God had so blessed us. Now at last we could travel together with relative comfort and ease. From the time we obtained the vehicle, invitations to speak started to come. Since then, we have shared in churches and groups across the nation. Travelling in one of the most beautiful countries in the world is no hardship. Wherever we go, we tell people about hope, and find a great response to this message. And I still believe that God will overtake us with healing. He has begun to fulfill the dream given so many years earlier, and at the time of writing has started to open the doors to minister in other nations.

Some months after starting to travel, we were invited to become part of a large and growing church in another part of Auckland. After being involved for seventeen years in the leadership of our previous church, it was hard to leave the people; however, a fresh season had begun. We sold our home, shifted across the city, and had a new home built by a very helpful building company. A week after we moved, I taught in our new church for four weekends while the pastor was overseas. The tree of life had sprouted. Hope had returned, and I wanted to see it restored to others who had lost it. I began to think about the things that cause hope to grow. The following is not an exhaustive list but are some of the ways God uses to create or restore hope.

His Word

The apostle Paul wrote, *"I pray also that the eyes of your heart may be enlightened in order that you may know the hope to which he has called you."* [4] It takes revelation to appreciate the hope God calls us to have. *"Man shall not live by bread alone,"* the Lord told Moses, *"but by every word that proceeds from the mouth of God."* [5] Jesus quoted this statement when being tempted by Satan to be self-sufficient. *"Make bread for yourself out of these stones,"* the devil challenged Jesus. [6] Jesus refused, but today many are trying to do just this, under the guise of secular humanism. Humanism is self-sufficiency. It is people living by bread alone.

Today secular humanism and its child, relativism, are sweeping western nations and governments. This worldview holds that humanity determines its own destiny, it is supreme, and truth is whatever is acceptable to the majority at any given time. Laws change to suit the prevailing belief, because there are no absolutes in humanism. The idea of a God to whom we must give account and an absolute moral code is repugnant to the humanist. Pluralism (the acceptance of all beliefs so that one does not impose itself on another) and tolerance are in – except, it seems, towards followers of Christ. The world has become grey. Where there is no word from heaven, there can be no hope.

Humanism and naturalism (the view that says that we are here by natural evolutionary processes) have robbed multitudes of hope. Eternity becomes an unknown: a black hole of nonexistence to some, or possibly a heaven, but certainly no hell, to others. Consequently, they live only for the present, for status, and for the material pleasures they feel will offer comfort from the pains of life. In other parts of the world, poverty, war and political instability have impoverished many, crushing their hopes of a decent life. As well, the strutting Goliath of radical Islam, with its sword of terrorism, has caused many to cower in despair.

Society is reaping from such hopelessness a terrible harvest of crime, violence, addictions, abuse and worse. Many are partying like there is no tomorrow. 'Eat, drink and be merry' has become their philosophy. However, we cannot live on bread – material goods and pleasures – alone. Though needed for living, and though God richly supplies us with all things to enjoy, they cannot be the source of life. Only God and his Word are.

The Bible, the Word of God, is God's revelation to humankind. It is the Word that has come from His mouth. It speaks of our origins, our disconnection from God, the way of reconnection to him through the Saviour, and our glorious future destiny. God has a future and a hope for all those who put their faith in him. If we intentionally and methodically read the Scriptures, asking the Holy Spirit for understanding, we will be strong in hope. If we are casual about the Word of God, we will struggle to have hope.

Revelation comes through the Bible. It also comes through prophecy, impressions from the Holy Spirit, visions and dreams. God can speak to us by many means but never violates the Scriptures. He speaks to give us direction, reveal himself, refine us and inspire hope. He also speaks to restore hope when it is lost.

As I sought God for revelation in my season of disillusionment, light began to come. The things I heard, many of which form the contents of this book, encouraged me to have hope. I believe the season is changing and if your heart has become sick because of deferred hope, be encouraged. Hold on to God, because he does want to fulfill the desires He has placed in your heart.

Power of the Holy Spirit

"Can these bones live?" the Lord asked the prophet Ezekiel. [7] Ezekiel had just seen a vision of an arid valley covered with the dried bones of a long dead army. After prophesying the words the Lord gave him, Ezekiel stared with astonishment as the bones re-assembled, and became

covered with muscles, flesh and skin. However, the army lay lifeless. It was not until Ezekiel prophesied to the wind, that the breath of God entered the bodies and they came alive and stood on their feet. The key was the breath of God. The breath of God is none other than the Spirit of God. On the Day of Pentecost, He came like a mighty, rushing wind and filled the disciples in Jerusalem. [8]

The Lord then revealed the entire point of this vision when He said, *"Son of man, these bones represent the people of Israel. They are saying, 'We have become old, dry bones – all hope is gone."* [9] They were in exile in Babylon. God promised that he would restore them to their homeland. It looked impossible. So did a valley of dry bones.

The vision of the dry bones demonstrates God's ability to resurrect hope in a dry season when it has eroded or died completely. Often hope dies because we enter the valley of trouble and fail to find the doorway of hope God promises to give us. [10] Trapped there, the valley of trouble becomes the valley of dry bones – dreams, hopes, and desires lie dead and decayed on the arid valley floor. When hope has died, we need the Spirit of God to fill us, and we need to hear the prophetic voice that declares that what was dead can live. The key is the prophetic and the breath of God – Word and Spirit.

"May the God of hope," says the New Testament, *"fill you with all joy and peace as you trust in him, so that you may overflow with hope by the power of the Holy Spirit."* [11] Some think the Holy Spirit is a power to get hold of and use to serve God. Rather he is a person who desires to get hold of us and to use us. We cannot have a relationship with a force; we can with a person. Intimacy with the Holy Spirit enables us to walk in hope. [12]

Hardship

"We also rejoice in our sufferings because we know that suffering produces perseverance; perseverance, character, and character, hope" [13] This is one of the most reflective statements that Paul the Apostle wrote. The greater the pain, the greater the hope, if we choose not to become bitter. If we persevere, suffering develops godly character, and godly character will cause us to be unashamed at the coming of the Lord, inspiring hope in that day. Perseverance is the key.

Paul knew what he was talking about. Speaking of the terrible and ongoing persecution he encountered in Asia, he wrote to the Christians in Corinth. *"We were under great pressure far beyond our ability to endure,"* he said, *"but this happened so that we might not rely on ourselves but on God who raises the dead... on him we have set our hope that he will continue to deliver us."* [14]

As he looked back, Paul could say these things in the same breath. However, at the time it may have taken awhile to realise what God was accomplishing through the pressure. Paul finally understood why the hardship had come and hope grew stronger as a result. If in our trials, we are able to say, *"But this happened so that..."* then we will gain God's perspective and hope will grow. Suffering, if handled correctly, produces hope. This is so important, and yet so often misunderstood, that I will devote the next two chapters to look at it.

Inner Healing

Life will wound us. Rash and unkind words spoken by parents, teachers, peers and others when we are young can injure the soul. Abusive actions and our own mistakes can further compound the wound. Unhealed wounds imprison us in past hurts and disappointments and prevent hope.

When God restores hope, he will address the scars of our soul. We may find ourselves having flashbacks to painful incidents. Often, this is the Holy Spirit's signal that he wants to heal these areas of our lives. Hope is a confident expectation of future good. When bitterness, unforgiveness or pain from the past is present, it is difficult to have that expectation.

It is not within the scope of this book to deal with this subject in detail. Many fine courses and books are available to help. [15] Talking with a trained Christian counsellor can also be of benefit. Ultimately, it is the healing ministry of the Holy Spirit that brings a person to wholeness.

Take a Risk

To hope is to risk. Hope is risky because you may set yourself up for disappointment. However, it is better to hope and be disappointed than not to hope at all. *"Hope in reality is the worst of all evils,"* said the controversial German philosopher Frederick Nietzsche, [16] *"because it prolongs the torments of man."* Nietzsche popularised the saying, *'God is dead.'* With no God and no hope, negativity and torment characterised his life and he died insane. Living without hope is a dangerous thing.

God said through the prophet Zechariah, *"Come back to the place of safety, all you prisoners, for there is yet hope! I promise this very day that I will repay you two mercies for each of your woes!"* [17] If we lose hope, it is dangerous, for the glasses of cynicism will taint our vision of everything. We must come back to the place of safety – the place of hope – and let it captivate us. God says he will give two mercies for every woe.

I will never forget a young couple in our last church. Ant and Nina were interns on the church staff. One of the pastors had approached a school that was located in a community with a very low socioeconomic rating. The school had experienced difficulty with many of its students, who were struggling with their learning. Some children were also getting into trouble after school due to the lack of activities accessible to them within the community. This pastor asked the principal for permission to help. On the condition that the assistance would not be of short duration, the principal agreed. The church asked Ant and Nina to lead this ministry into the school.

As they and their team began to assist the school, God gave them an expanding vision. Remedial reading, home-work groups, after school clubs, performing and visual arts groups, sponsorship for computers and other equipment all contributed to the children's blossoming. As the ministry developed, Ant and Nina's commitment grew. To be more available to the children, they left a lovely home in a pleasant suburb and lived beside the school in a home that was very basic.

Now for many years, they had wanted to have children of their own, but Nina could not conceive. Finally, after a long time trying, she became pregnant. About two months into the pregnancy, she started to bleed and was rushed into hospital. All through the night, it was touch and go. Scheduled to go to church the next day and communicate what he and Nina were doing in the school, Ant agonised over whether to go or stay with his wife. Nina encouraged him to go, to tell the people about the children and the help they needed. He went. She lost the baby. They were heartbroken. Nevertheless, they kept pouring themselves out for the children of others.

A few years later, Nina became pregnant again, and discovered she had twins. She eventually gave birth to a boy and a girl! When God says, *"I will give you two mercies for every woe,"* He really means it. As one of my friends likes to say, *"He gives you double for your trouble."* Now some stories do not end up like this, but in eternity, they will – if not here on earth.

The apostle Peter said, *"Prepare your minds for action; be self-controlled; set your hope **fully** on the grace to be given you when Jesus Christ is revealed."* [18] In the original Greek language of the New Testament, the word 'fully' means 'completely, without wavering, and to the end.' [19] To have complete and unwavering hope to the end will be worth it when Jesus returns.

Saved by a Piece of Chocolate

A friend tells the story of her father who was a prisoner of war during World War II.

"When I was little," she says, "I would go fishing with my father. I didn't like fishing but I liked him! So I went. It seemed we sat forever in the boat waiting. It would get dark and cold and I would feel that it must be time to go home. He had an understanding of timing that belonged to a father and his child. At just the right moment, he would delve into the pocket of his oilskin coat and produce on his outstretched hand a single square of chocolate. He presented it as though I was the most honoured of children and I would wait until he had turned back to his rod to wipe the 'extra bits' off it.

He had been an officer in charge of men in the Second World War. Captured in the North African desert, they endured things I was never to hear. He told me that sometimes in the prison camp one of his men would begin to die. They were starving and ill,

63

but he said the worst thing was when they had lost hope.

Occasionally, Red Cross parcels made their way through and my father would hide the chocolate. At some point, he would offer the dying soldier a single square that somehow seemed to condense hope and give him the will to go on. That a man would choose life from such a small token offered to him impressed itself indelibly on my small person."

God is the restorer of hope. One small square of chocolate restored a man's hope and helped him live. How much greater are the processes God uses to restore hope in his children.

Notes

[1] G.K. Chesterton, Christian author and apologist (1874-1936).

2 Proverbs 13:12a (RSV)

[3] Ecclesiastes 11:4

[4] Ephesians 1:18 (NIV)

[5] Deuteronomy 8:3 (NIV)

[6] Matthew 4:3 (NIV)

[7] Ezekiel 37:3 (NIV)

[8] Acts 2

[9] Ezekiel 37:11

[10] Hosea 2:15

[11] Romans 15:13 (NIV)

[12] To understand more about the Holy Spirit and how to know him, see *Going Deeper with the Holy Spirit* by Benny Hinn, Dallas, Clarion Call Marketing Inc., 2005.

[13] Romans 5:3,4 (NIV)

[14] 2 Corinthians 1:8-10 (NIV)

[15] See for example, *Created for Love* and *Created to be Whole* by John & Agnes Sturt, Guilford, Surrey, Eagle Publishing, 1994 & 1998 respectively.

[16] Frederick Nietzsche (1844 – 1900)

[17] Zechariah 9:12

[18] 1 Peter 1:13 (NIV)

[19] Strong's 5049

Chapter Six

Why Do Bad Things Happen to Good People?

"To live is to suffer,
To survive is to find some meaning
In the suffering." [1]

In the previous chapter, we saw that suffering is one means God uses to produce hope. Bad things happen to good people and this can be difficult to handle. But handle it we must, for if we don't, the circumstances designed to create hope will instead produce bitterness.

Some time ago, I preached at a church in mourning. A few days earlier, one of their youth leaders had died in a vehicle accident. This lovely young woman and her fiancé were travelling home from the hospital where they had just visited her dying grandfather. Ahead of them and unseen, a motorcyclist, pursued by police, travelled toward them at high speed. The rider rounded a corner, lost control of his bike, and slammed into their vehicle, killing himself and gravely injuring the young woman, who died a short time later. Her fiancé was spared. The tragic incident received widespread coverage in the news. But the family's faith shone out in this difficult time, while many people, including fellow church members, asked, *"Why?"*

Why did this terrible event have to happen? Why do bad things happen to good people? Why is there so much suffering in the world? Failure to give a reasonable account of these questions can destroy hope, resulting in disappointment or resentment that creates a barrier between God and us. I have seen many who begin in hope, encounter heart-breaking circumstances, and throw away their confidence in God. Surveys show that one of the greatest obstacles to someone's coming to faith in God is the unanswered question, *"If God is a loving God, why is there so much suffering in the world?"* Christians need to have answers for this and similar questions.

It seems much more straightforward to explain why bad things happen to bad people. That, we say, is justice. We even accept it when good things happen to bad people. That is the mercy of God. However, it takes a more searching effort to understand why bad things happen to good people. *"It is the glory of God to conceal a matter; to search out a matter is the glory of kings."* [2]

So what are some of the explanations for this troubling question? Over the years, I have learned a few, but by no means all, of them. In fact, only eternity will reveal answers to some situations. In the Western church we have too often embraced clever formulae for living, and lost our sense of the awe and wonder of God. We try to reduce God to predictable patterns of behaviour. We want answers and we want them now. Part of Christian maturity is to learn to live with mystery – to live patiently with a situation for which an explanation may not come for years or even a lifetime.

A pastor friend of mine lost his wife after a seven-year battle with cancer. They prayed for healing, but she died. Naturally, he asked the question, *"Why didn't God heal her? Why did we have to go through all those years of struggle?"* Eventually, my friend concluded, *"Like Job I have come through a time of suffering only to find that God owes me no answers. He strengthens me, encourages me, anoints me, empowers me, but the question, 'Why?' remains unanswered."* Despite the lack of answers, he has chosen to live with mystery and keep his trust in God intact.

There may not be an answer to everything in this life, but in eternity, there will be. However, some reasons do make sense here and now.

We Live in a Fallen World

Firstly, this world is not the way God made it. When the first man and woman sinned, a curse came into the world. Hardship, violence, disease, genetic abnormalities, environmental upheavals, poverty and hunger all trace their origins to this fall from the perfect order and harmony of the original creation. One day Jesus will restore everything to perfection in a new heaven and earth. Until he does, tragedies will occur because we live on a broken planet.

People Have Free Will

One of God's most precious gifts to humanity is free will, which he will not violate. This means there are times people will decide to do bad things to us and we will suffer the consequences of their decisions. God sometimes steps in to protect us, yet at other times he chooses not to. At times, our own decisions bring painful consequences of their own and yet we may blame God. The Bible says, *"People ruin their lives by their own foolishness and then are angry at the Lord."* [3]

Satan is Alive and Active

Another obvious reason for suffering is the Devil, or Satan. Satan is a fallen archangel who leads an army of evil spirits in rebellion against God. Jesus called him a murderer, a thief and a liar. He kills, steals and deceives. Sooner or later we will get caught up in this spiritual battle. Until God finally casts him into hell at the end of time, Satan will continue to deceive the nations, seeking to destroy the lives of men and women made in the image of God.

Anointed by God, Jesus went about doing good and *"healing all who were oppressed by the devil."* [4] For example, when Jesus healed a woman crippled by an evil spirit – she was bent double and had been unable to stand up straight for many years – he remarked, *"Wasn't it necessary for me...to free this dear woman from the bondage in which Satan has held her for eighteen years?"* [5] When the church is alert to this spiritual war, and prays and does the works that Jesus did, it forbids Satan to oppress and destroy people, families, cities and nations.

God Wants to Make Us Like His Son

This fourth reason is the focus of this chapter and is often the most perplexing to understand. The apostle Paul said, *"We know that God causes everything to work together for the good of those who love God and are called according to his purpose for them. For God knew his people in advance, and chose them to become like his Son."* [6]

God works everything for good. This is easy to believe when something good happens. However, it is harder to believe when tragedy strikes, relationships fall apart, finance is lacking, sickness remains or rape or abuse occurs. In these circumstances Satan will come and accuse God just as he did in the Garden of Eden. When God looks bad, sin looks good and we will be tempted to doubt God's goodness and love. Right at this point the foundation of our faith can be undermined causing many to stumble. Some people abandon their faith in God, or become distant from him, because they cannot understand why a good God would allow bad things to happen to them.

No Matter What Happens, God is a Good God

It seems a contradiction, but I believe that we learn about the goodness of God better in the hard times than in the good times. During my battle with cancer, it wasn't until I came across the following verse from the psalms that I understood this: *"Before I was afflicted I went astray, but now I obey your word. You are good and what you do is good...It was good for me that I was afflicted, so that I might learn your decrees."* [7] This amazed me. The writer actually states that affliction was good for him. Not only that, but he declares that both God's character and actions are good.

Obedience is learned in affliction. Hardship can be a very effective teacher. The book of Hebrews says, *"Even though Jesus was God's son, he learned obedience from the things he suffered."* [8] If Jesus, then us. This is the pattern for the shaping of our lives. While God uses many things to shape us, hardship gets our attention the most. C.S. Lewis wrote, *"God whispers to us in our pleasures, speaks in our conscience, but shouts in our pains."* [9] The Bible confirms this by stating, *"By means of their suffering, [God] rescues those who suffer. For he gets their attention through adversity."* [10]

When we learn obedience through what we suffer, we become more like the Son of God. The apostle James put it like this: *"Whenever trouble comes your way, let it be an opportunity for joy. For when your faith is tested, your endurance has a chance to grow. So let it grow, for when your endurance is fully developed, you will be strong in character and ready for anything."* [11]

Often the joy is not apparent there and then, for it takes time to see the good that God is producing in us. As we look back, sometimes years later, it may be only then that we realise the full extent of the transformation God has produced within us. Whatever suffering we may encounter, we must cling to the declaration, *"You are good, and what You do is good."*

The Holocaust

The Holocaust is a clear example in recent history where God turned something evil to good. The Nazis murdered nearly six million Jews in Hitler's death camps during World War II. This was the raw face of evil. Did God send the Holocaust? No. In an attempt to frustrate God's purposes by annihilating God's covenant people, the Jews, Satan conceived it and drove a willing Hitler to do it. God permitted it, just as he permitted his Son to be crucified. Evil had apparently triumphed.

Yet out of this horror, came the formation of the nation of Israel in 1948, in miraculous fulfillment of prophecy. Because of the great evil the Jews had suffered, the world was sympathetic to them and agreed to the formation of the modern state of Israel. If there had been no Holocaust, there would be no Israel today.

The Storm

As another example, the book of Acts records that as the apostle Paul sailed to Rome to stand trial before Caesar, the boat he was in became caught in a hurricane-force storm in the Mediterranean Sea. Adrift for at least two weeks in the open sea, the boat was continuously lashed by violent waves and fierce winds and the 275 persons aboard gave up all hope of rescue. All except Paul! Claiming an angel had given him a message from God, he said, *"Take courage! None of you will lose your lives, even though the ship will go down. For last night an angel of the God to whom I belong and whom I serve stood beside me, and he said, 'Don't be afraid Paul, for you will surely stand trial before Caesar! What's more, God in his goodness has granted safety to everyone sailing with you'. So take courage! For I believe God. It will be just as he said. But we will be shipwrecked on an island."* [12]

The angel's message was not exactly encouraging: the ship would go down, Paul would stand trial before Caesar, and they would be shipwrecked. But the heavenly messenger also promised that 'God in his goodness' would spare all their lives. God in his goodness? They were in a ferocious storm! Men and angels see things very differently. It is often hard to find any trace of God's goodness in the middle of a storm of trouble. It requires heaven's perspective. God, in his goodness, may not keep us from the storm, but will see us through it. He is good, and what he does is good.

From Tragedy to Triumph

It was the early 1950's. The young couple had just been married. On their honeymoon both contracted polio, which left them paralysed and confined to wheelchairs. Despite the difficulties, they had a family, raised their children, worked and ran a business. As the couple's two sons, Trevor and Wayne, grew, they observed the difficulty their parents faced when having to enter and exit vehicles. An idea dawned of creating a vehicle in which disabled persons could travel more easily.

Inspired by a vehicle customized overseas, the brothers designed and engineered a vehicle that a wheelchair user could access as either a passenger or driver, without having to leave his or her wheelchair. Their business, Vehicle Adaption Services,[13] has gone on to produce many such vehicles, one of which is the vehicle Jane and I use to keep our ministry mobile. We now have a freedom undreamed of a few years ago. Out of their parents' misfortune, these two brothers have created something that is dramatically changing the lives of many disabled people.

Joseph

In the Old Testament, Joseph is a further wonderful example of discovering God's goodness in the midst of adversity. At seventeen, he had a dream about his family bowing down to him. Unwisely, he shared it with them. This was premature as he did not have the character or humility to handle the revelation God had given him. In fact, Joseph was arrogant. The favoured son of Jacob, he already felt superior to his brothers, and the dream reinforced that feeling. His brothers hated him even more and sold him as a slave into Egypt.

Thirteen years later, after working as a slave, and being falsely accused of a rape that sent him to prison, he was made prime minister of Egypt. He interpreted Pharaoh's dream about an impending famine, and recommended a brilliant administrative strategy to cope with the crisis. Seven or so years later, when the famine had become severe, his brothers came to Egypt to purchase food, and bowed down to him as ruler of the land. In all, it took some twenty years for the dream to be fulfilled. The Psalms say, *"Until the time came to fulfill his word, the Lord tested Joseph's character."* [14] Joseph passed the test. He had learned obedience through what he suffered. He had also learned that God was working something good in the situation. After their father Jacob died, Joseph reassured his brothers of his forgiveness of them by saying, *"As far as I am concerned, God turned into good what you meant for evil. He brought me to this high position I have today so I could save the lives of many people."* [15]

It was clear to Joseph that *'God is good, and what he does is good.'* In fact, the names he gave to his two sons, born in Egypt, are revealing. One he called Manasseh, which means, *'God has made me forget all my troubles.'* The other he named Ephraim, which means *'God has made me fruitful in this land of my suffering.'*

In confinement, there is always refinement if we endure. Afterwards, God will make us forget and make us fruitful. *"And the God of all grace, who called you to his eternal glory in Christ, after you have suffered a little while, will himself restore you, and make you strong, firm, and steadfast."* [16] Now the Bible's 'little while' may be a few months or it may be a lifetime. God's ultimate purposes are greater than our present comfort. His goodness does not guarantee our immediate comfort and in our pain we must trust him.

Finding God

Christian counsellor and author Dr. Larry Crabb has said, *"Feeling better has become more important than finding God. Finding God means to face all life, both good and bad, with a spirit of trust ... You know you are finding God when you believe that God is good no matter what happens."* [17]

As an illustration, consider divine healing. Healing is perfectly available through the cross of Christ, but at times imperfectly ministered or received. We do not yet see everyone who receives prayer, healed. I have hope that will change. [18] Sometimes, people appear to do everything right in believing for healing, and still it does not come. It is then that we need to accept the mysterious in our walk with God, and bow to him. We should not, however, reduce our theology about healing to the level of our circumstances, or doubt God's goodness or willingness to heal. A friend of mine, commenting on divine healing, said recently, *"We have been so afraid of giving people false hope, that we have given them no hope at all."* He is the God who forgives all our sins and heals all our diseases. [19] That is why I do not believe that my wife's sickness is from God. It is a terrible disease and originates from a more sinister source. [20] However, God is working great good in the situation, and we are finding him, while we wait expectantly for healing.

Sometime ago, I asked my wife what she had learned all the years she has been in a wheelchair. Jane surprised me with her answer. She said, *"I've learned to smile."* In the midst of her suffering, she has discovered God's goodness. Wherever we go, people comment on her smile and the sparkle in her eyes. The eyes are the window of the soul. Deep in her soul, Jane has learned to maintain hope because she knows God is good and what He does is good. She has chosen to take the long view.

Take the Long View

How do we cope when bad things happen to us? How do we keep going? How do we forgive? We have to take the long view. If we take the short view, we will try to balance everything in this life. The ledger of good and bad will not always balance in this life, but in eternity it will. *"So be truly glad!"* says the Bible. *"There is wonderful joy ahead, even though it is necessary for you to endure many trials for a while. These trials are only to test your faith, to show that it is strong and pure. It is being tested as fire tests and purifies gold – and your faith is far more precious to God than mere gold. So if your faith remains strong after being tried by fiery trials, it will bring you much praise and glory and honour on the day when Jesus Christ is revealed to the whole world."* [21]

Notes

1 Roberta Flack, singer and songwriter (1937 -)
2 Proverbs 25:2 (NIV)
3 Proverbs 19:3
4 Acts 10:38 (NIV)
5 Luke 13:10-17.
6 Romans 8:28,29a
7 Psalm 119:67,68a,71 (NIV)
8 Hebrews 5:8
9 *The Problem of Pain*, New York, HarperCollins Publishers, 2001, p.91. (First published 1940).
10 Job 36:15
11 James 1:3,4
12 Acts 27:22-26
14 See www.vas.co.nz
15 Psalm 105:19
16 Genesis 50:20
17 1 Peter 5:10 (NIV)
18 *Finding God*, Grand Rapids, Zondervan Publishing House, 1993, p.17
19 At the time of writing, there are already worldwide signs of a fresh move of the Holy Spirit in supernatural healings and miracles.
19 Psalm 103: 3
20 There are rare times when God does send sickness as a judgment for wrongdoing (see for example Numbers 12:9-11, Acts 12:23, Revelation 2:20-22). There are also times when we may bring sickness upon ourselves due to disregarding healthy dietary and lifestyle principles. However, I believe that the vast majority of

sickness is due to Satanic affliction, and living in a fallen, diseased world. The extensive healing ministry of Jesus provides conclusive evidence of God's attitude to sickness.

[21] 1 Peter 1 :6,7

Chapter Seven

The Prayer Most Christians Avoid

"It was the season of light;
it was the season of darkness,

It was the spring of hope;
it was the winter of despair." [1]

God is good and what he does is good. And there is a good that God works in adversity that is profoundly great – the gift of fellowship with his Son in his sufferings. *"I want to know Christ,"* said the apostle Paul, *"and the power of his resurrection and the fellowship of sharing in his sufferings, becoming like him in his death, and so, somehow to attain to the resurrection from the dead."* [2]

The Fellowship of His Sufferings

Many believers happily pray to know Christ and the power of his resurrection; not so many pray to know the fellowship of his sufferings. What does this mean? How is it possible to partner with Christ in his sufferings? I once thought that it meant we would know his closeness when we suffer, and he would comfort and empathise with us. This is true, but only half the story. Some years ago, I became aware of what the fullness of this means.

For some time, the sense of loss caused by my wife's illness, had overcome me. My mind drifted back to the summer of our wedding; it was as happy a day as any I have experienced, when sickness was a world away and Jane exuded health. It saddened me that she could now no longer walk, or hold my hand as we strolled on the beach, or stand and minister with me. I had prayed for healing many times, but one day, in my pain, cried out, *"Lord, I want my bride back!"* What happened next sliced straight through my self-pity.

Jesus spoke to me. Into my mind came words that were so clear, they seemed audible. He replied, *"I know what you feel – I want my bride back too!"* I suddenly felt the ache in his heart for the church. She is his bride, purchased with a great price. In his letter to the Corinthians, the apostle Paul said, *"I promised you as a pure bride to one husband, Christ. But I fear somehow you will be led away from your pure and simple devotion to Christ, just as Eve was deceived by the serpent."* [3] While Jesus loves his church as she is, it pains him when she is weak or has lost her first love. He wants a healthy bride – one that is empowered and radically in love with him. As such we will better radiate him to a world that has lost its way, a world he deeply cares for. In that moment of revelation, I realised he understood my distress, and in some small way, I understood his. I knew an intimacy with him in our mutual pain, which I had never experienced before. This was fellowshipping in his sufferings.

Pain can be a gift that allows us to glimpse God's heart, listening for the things that grieve him. However, instead of hearing his voice, we can be deafened by the loudness of our pain. Many walk away from this opportunity of intimacy, so focused on their own suffering that they fail to feel his. It is not that the Lord wants to minimise our distress or overlook it. In fact, the book of Hebrews says, *"We do not have a high priest who is unable to understand and sympathise and have fellow feeling with our weaknesses and infirmities."* [4] Rather, it is as one pastor said, *"Every situation of pain is an invitation into the heart of Jesus."*

Whatever we are suffering, Jesus suffered more. He knows. He will walk with us. He will share secrets with us. We will discover things about him we would not learn in any other way. When we fellowship in his sufferings in this way, we get to know him better. This gives meaning to the painful things we may go through in life. I will never forget what he said to me when I cried out to him. It has brought an intimacy I could know in no other way. That alone has made the pain worth it.

The Power of His Resurrection

Knowing Christ is to know not only the fellowship of his sufferings, but also the power of his resurrection. As these appear to be opposites, we may embrace one over the other. But in holding both together, we mature.

The power of Christ's resurrection is the mighty power by which he will one day raise dead believers from the grave and give them glorious new bodies – bodies that will never sin, become sick, or die. This is a wonderful hope for all Christians, especially those who are afflicted in this life. However, the power of his resurrection also refers to the Holy Spirit releasing God's power in this present life to effect salvation, deliverance and healing. We experienced this power when God healed Jane from lifelong migraine headaches.

Hence, for years, my wife and I have sought God for healing from Multiple Sclerosis, but nothing has happened yet. We have discovered that at times, he may allow us to live with a mysterious tension: tension between his power to intervene in our lives and the painful, daily reality of unchanged circumstances. Accepting this is to know God at a deeper level. We learn to recognize his paradoxes. When we are weak, then we are strong. When we die to self, we live.

So much of Christianity seems to be either/or today. We tend to polarise around a moral issue or biblical truth, and fail to understand that God uses opposites to mature us. Or if it is not either/or, it is some bland flavour of truth halfway between – a watered down belief justified as 'balance'. Rather, we need to passionately embrace the full range of truth, even when that range includes apparent opposites. We should not, as a pastor friend stated, *"be ruled by the tyranny of the 'or', but the genius of the 'and'."* God desires that, *"we will be mature and full grown in the Lord, measuring up to the full stature of Christ."* [5] The Lord is multidimensional; we, however, often take one of his dimensions and call it his fullness.

For example, a few years ago, I asked the Lord for a theme for the coming year. That day, I read a verse from Psalm 37. It said, *"Don't be impatient for the Lord to act! Travel steadily along his path."* [6] This spoke to me – I saw the need for patient, steady endurance. Later in the day, a friend, who is a prophet, telephoned me. He told me that he had a message for me. It was from the book of Malachi and it said, *"The Lord you are seeking will come suddenly to his temple."* [7] In other words, I should expect the sudden and sovereign interventions of God in my life.

As these verses appeared to contradict each other, I assumed one of us had not heard God correctly. When I asked the Holy Spirit about it, he simply said, *"Both are correct. Too many of my people want my suddenlies, without being willing to walk steadily. If they will walk steadily, and seek me, there will be suddenlies.*" Steadily and suddenly. The former inspires perseverance, while the latter inspires hope. Grasping both has greatly helped Jane and me to cope with our circumstances. Another case of opposites held in tension, these two truths become most powerful when put together: *"Don't be impatient for the Lord to act! Travel steadily along his path...and the Lord you are seeking will come suddenly to his temple."*

This example of steadily/suddenly is similar to the fellowship of his sufferings and the power of his resurrection. Though apparent opposites, we need to embrace them both. God is the One who sustains us in adversity, giving value to our pain as we share in the sufferings of his Son. However, he is also our healer and deliverer. It is possible to passively accept suffering and exclude the possibility of release. Too many put up with sickness and affliction under the guise of 'suffering for God', when they need to trust in Christ's resurrection power to free them. [8]

On the other hand, in our pursuit of healing or deliverance, we can become impatient and miss the joys of intimacy with him in adversity. As we hold both together, we can continue to have faith for release, whilst journeying deeper, through our pain and difficulties, into his heart. There we come to a place of sensitivity to, and intimacy with, him. The writer of the following worship song captured this well:

When your heart beats, I want to feel it;

When your voice speaks, I want to hear it;

When your eyes cry, I want to catch the tears;

I want to know you. [9]

"Dear friends," said the apostle Peter, *"don't be surprised at the fiery trials you are going through, as if something strange were happening to you. Instead, be very glad – because these trials will make you partners with Christ in his suffering, and afterward you will have the wonderful joy of sharing his glory when it is displayed to the world."* [10]

One day, the Father will reveal the full glory of his Son to the world. At that time, those who share the sufferings of Christ will share in that glory. If we fellowship in his sufferings, then we will also fellowship in his glory.

That is our hope in adversity!

Notes

[1] Charles Dickens, British classical author (1812 – 1870)

[2] Philippians 3:10,11 (NIV)

[3] 2 Corinthians 11: 2,3

[4] Hebrews 4:15 (Amplified)

[5] Ephesians 4:13b

[6] Psalm 37:34a

[7] Malachi 3:1

[8] Even if we have waited for years, we should continue to trust in God, and not yield to disappointment. Many of the sick people Jesus and the disciples healed had been ill for years or even a lifetime. Then one day freedom suddenly came. (See for example Mark 5:25-29; John 5:5-9; John 9:1-7; Acts 3:2-8; Acts 9:33-34; Acts 14:8-10)

[9] Verse one, *I Want to Know You* by Darrell Evans, © Integrity's Hosanna Music/ASCAP, 1997.

[10] 1 Peter 4:12,13

Jane and David on their wedding day.

Jane with Joseph, born three months premature.

*From left: Joseph, Tim, and Adam,
prior to David contracting cancer.*

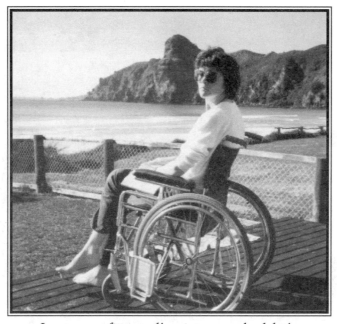

Jane soon after needing to use a wheelchair.

Jane and David today.

*From left: Tim, David with grandson Jordan,
Jane, Adam, and Joseph*

PART TWO

HOPE THAT WORKS

I believe that hope and work are inseparably linked. The Bible reveals that our deeds or works will follow us into eternity. There, good deeds and worthy work will be wonderfully rewarded, and worthless works consumed. *"But there is going to come a time of testing at the Judgment Day to see what kind of work each builder has done,"* said the apostle Paul, *"Everyone's work will be put through the fire to see whether or not it keeps its value. If the work survives the fire, the builder will receive a reward, but if the work is burned up, the builder will suffer great loss. The builders themselves will be saved but like someone escaping through a wall of flames."* [1]

Paul describes here the judgment of believers at the end of time – it is a judgment not of punishment, but of reward. Now, we really would have to live very carelessly to obtain no reward at all. Yet many do so, not wilfully, but by failing to understand what constitutes work that merits reward. Earth notices stars; heaven notices servants. Many feel hopeless because they rate what they do through earth's eyes and it seems insignificant. Instead, we must learn to extract hope from the seeming mundaneness of everyday life. No matter how small or tedious, work done in faith, hope, and love – for these endure [2] – is pleasing to God.

In order to care for my wife, I resigned from fulltime Christian service – something that represents the ultimate type of work to many believers. I struggled doing so, because I felt that my new role was not as significant as my previous one. I was looking merely through human eyes. As I came to see the importance of all good work, I saw purpose and value in what I did, that it pleased God and He would reward it. And that gave me hope.

The following chapters explore the connection between work and hope, define what worthy work really is, expose the flawed Western view of work, and consider the link between work and worship.

Notes
[1] 1 Corinthians 3:13-15
[2] 1 Corinthians 13:13

Chapter Eight

Your Work Has Value

"Blessed is he who has found his work;
Let him ask no other blessedness.
He has a work, a life purpose." [1]

It is one of the best selling books of all time in the United States. *"The Purpose Driven Life"* [2] by Rick Warren, a devotional that encourages people to live purpose-filled lives, has sold millions of copies worldwide. This should be no surprise. In a world where pop culture urges people to live for their own pleasures, many long for a higher sense of purpose to give greater meaning to their lives. With purpose comes hope – the expectation that our lives will count for something good in an empty world. And purpose is consistently linked with having some valuable or important work to do. Thus, hope and work are connected. Hope, we have discovered, is a confident expectation of good. What greater good is there than to bring pleasure to God in the work we do, bless others, and know that one day He will reward such work in eternity? That's why, if we have no valuable work to do, hope dies. I experienced this in 1986 during my battle with cancer.

At that time, the disease gradually forced me to give up my pastoral duties. Chemotherapy sapped all my strength, and the cocktail of drugs made it difficult to concentrate. I could barely pray or read my Bible, let alone perform any other pastoral work. This worsened over the course of the treatment, until I could do almost nothing. I felt hopeless. One day, I sat in my office, and stared at the wall. Frustration simmered within me until I finally protested, *"Lord, I feel so bored and unfulfilled!"*

Now I expected some comfort in return; however, that is not what I received. God comforts our pain, not our complaints. Quietly but clearly the Lord said, *"That is exactly how many of my people feel."* This jolted me. Could it really be that other believers felt like I did? This began to open my eyes; they would open more completely some years later. At the time, I assumed that the solution to this problem was to find everyone a role in the life of the church, based on his or her gifts and abilities. This was to prove illusive and frustrating. Clearly, I did not have all the answers then, but that day God planted fresh understanding in me.

Twelve years later, I recalled this event when my church was dealing with the aftermath of its pastor's unfortunate resignation. He had been a charismatic figure and the church had grown through his ministry and leadership. A large team of fulltime staff oversaw the diverse ministries and programs that operated within the church. Many people were fruitfully engaged in those ministries, because we stressed that all believers were ministers, not just the staff. Despite this, over the years a number of people had lost their enthusiasm and withdrawn. Were these people disloyal? Couldn't they see the vision we leaders had? It excited us – didn't it excite them? Therefore, we worked, preached, and cast the vision harder, but little changed. Clearly, until the pastor's sin was uncovered, the church was not going to move forward. However, I do not believe this was the only reason that the church struggled.

There seemed to be a major flaw in the whole structure. Something was missing from our understanding of church life. Sensing this, some of the younger leaders promoted a vision of people serving outside the congregation, which unsettled me. I thought if we could just have more meetings where God's presence was evident, everything would be all right. I am not sure why I believed this, because we had already enjoyed nearly four years of a powerful move of the Holy Spirit initiating from Toronto, Canada, yet the same frustrations about the church kept surfacing. Puzzled and disillusioned about the whole situation, I searched for understanding.

That is when the incident of 1986 flashed back to me. At the same time, the leadership team, questioning the philosophy of church life we had embraced, looked for a new way forward after our pastor's resignation. It dawned on us that the way many churches functioned forced people to be mere spectators. People accepted this for a time, taking in the sights and sounds that were new to many of them. However, after some years, the glow wore off and they too longed for some important work to do in God's Kingdom. We had unwittingly given the impression that such work was in 'full-time' Christian service or service in the congregation. While for some that remained true, many could not attain to this, and lost hope. Reduced to mere observer status, they became increasingly bored and unfulfilled, and a number finally withdrew. God was clearing our vision.

Michelangelo

In the Sistine Chapel at Rome are beautiful frescos by the renowned artist Michelangelo. Finished in the year 1512, they took Michelangelo five years to complete. The scenes he fashioned form a panorama of biblical history, from the creation of Adam to the return of the Lord. They are brilliant in their form and creativity. Art lovers the world over have long admired their original beauty. The creation of Adam scene alone is outstanding in its splendour and genius. A reclining Adam stretches out his hand to God whose own arm stretches towards Adam's. Creator and created reach for one another. Their index fingers almost touch, but not quite. God is not far from each one of us, said the apostle Paul; perhaps Michelangelo was capturing this thought.

Some, observing the rather muted colours of the fresco, had thought Michelangelo quite sombre. Perhaps this reflected the age in which he lived or his personality. In the 1990's church authorities painstakingly cleaned the frescos. On completion of the restoration, with nearly five hundred years of candle soot cleaned away, the difference was astonishing, even breathtaking. Everywhere, colours were vivid, and in some places almost garish. Rather than being sombre, the scenes were bright and revealed previously hidden details. This was not the Michelangelo many had been accustomed to. They complained that the cleaning had ruined the artist's work. Others felt they were seeing the true artist for the first time – this was the original as he had painted it.

So it is with the church. God is wiping away the accumulated dust and soot of years of culture and tradition, which dims the amazing and colourful truths of his Word. He is not painting a new picture so much as revealing the fullness of what is already there. One of the things he is bringing into colour and focus is the role of the believer in everyday life and the value of the work we are charged with doing. God is cleansing centuries of faulty thinking in order to create a hope-filled and purpose-filled generation, and for many, this will conflict with previously held views.

The Lord's Work

"So, my dear brothers and sisters," said the apostle Paul to the Corinthians, *"be strong and steady, always enthusiastic about the Lord's work, for you know that nothing you do for the Lord is ever useless."* [3] 'So' means because of what was said beforehand. Paul had just spoken of the resurrection of the dead, the ultimate triumph of Christ over all enemies, especially death, and about the future glory of believers. [4] Now he says that we are not to be escapists who dream of that future day and live carelessly. Rather, we are to work with purpose, abounding in the work of the Lord. The problem in understanding this scripture arises with what constitutes 'the Lord's work'. Is it full-time Christian service? Is it the work we perform in the congregation, or evangelism, or some ministry we exercise? It is definitely these, but it is also much broader in scope than these alone.

The modern Western Christian usually applies a kind of mental dualism to work. [5] That is, we classify work as sacred or secular. Ministry, for example, is sacred work; employment is secular work. This stems from the ancient Greek view of work. Nobody disputes that Greek and Roman thought has heavily influenced Western culture. The Greeks saw work as a curse. They had established a hierarchical society where landless men, women and slaves would do the work for them. Freed from work's dreary grip on their lives, they could focus on the two higher purposes of life: politics and contemplation (philosophy and spirituality). Theirs was a dualistic worldview.

The Hebrews, however, saw work and spirituality as equal ingredients in a meaningful life. Work in the fields was as important as worship in the temple. Theirs was a holistic worldview. An incident in the ministry of Jesus illustrates this. One Sabbath, He and the disciples walked through some wheat fields and, feeling hungry, the disciples began to pick some grain to eat. Observing this, certain Pharisees protested, *"It's against the law to work by harvesting grain on the Sabbath."* 6 Jesus dismissed their protest as inflexible legalism. Later the same day, Jesus noticed a man with a deformed hand. The ever-present Pharisees asked, *"Is it legal to work by healing on the Sabbath day?"* 7 Again, Jesus refuted their question and healed the man. Putting aside the Pharisees' blind legalism, we see that the Jews classed both harvesting grain and healing the sick as equivalent kinds of work.

Jesus and the apostle Paul, both being Hebrews, commended work in its general sense. At his baptism and after eighteen years working as a carpenter, and before he had become an itinerant preacher, Jesus heard his Father declare, *"You are my beloved Son, and I am fully pleased with you."* 8 For what reason? Obedience? Character? Certainly. However, could it be that the Father also took pleasure in the work Jesus had already done and the way he performed it? Undoubtedly, his powerful ministry as well as his death and resurrection were the things that changed the world forever. Nevertheless, I do not imagine Jesus the artisan despised his work while longing impatiently to become Jesus the Messiah. In fact, there is a scene in Mel Gibson's movie *"The Passion,"* which seems to capture this thought. A younger Jesus shows his mother a table he has constructed for a customer. Laughing with Mary over the unusual design, which has longer legs than normal for sitting rather than reclining at, Jesus takes obvious delight in his workmanship.

Dualism in the Church

Three hundred years after Jesus and Paul, Augustine, a noted church father of the time, wrote about the relative merits of contemplation and work. While Augustine claimed both kinds of life were good, he saw the contemplative life as superior. Influenced by the growing Greek thought in the church (this was around the time that Jewish Christians were excluded from the church unless they gave up all vestiges of Jewish practice), Augustine thus reinforced the dualistic view of work. Some work was holy; some was ordinary. Later, the monastic orders, many of whom gave themselves to agricultural work, practical service to the poor and so on, challenged this view.

Martin Luther, the great reformer, also disputed it. In his day, the church saw the work of its clergy as vastly superior to that of the common person. Luther however, praised the value of all work and all occupations. As one theologian has written, *"It was Luther who made popular the notion that housewives, farmers, butchers, bakers, and candlestick makers have callings just as high as those of professional clerics and monastics."* [9] Sadly, with overemphasis and the passing of time, the pursuit of a vocation became an end in itself, without any reference to the calling of God. Consequently, in much Protestant and Western thinking, work became secularised, a stand-alone thing apart from faith. And this divided thinking still exists amongst many believers today.

For example, leading a cell group is 'spiritual,' but employment is ordinary. Preaching for the pastor is greater than balancing the books for the accountant. Devotional activities such as reading the Bible and prayer are holier than manual work. [10] Some businesspeople have more responsibility and lead larger staffs than many pastors do, yet the significance of what they do is reduced to providing finance for the church, as important as that is. Conversely, many pastors frustrate themselves by trying to mobilize all the members to serve in the congregation, or in church-organised ministries to the community. Few will ever succeed, because the field of service is all of God's creation, not just the local church.

Pastor and Bible teacher Charles Simpson once said, *"I met a young man not long ago who dives for exotic fish for aquariums. He said one of the most popular aquarium fish is the shark. He explained that if you catch a small shark and confine it, it will stay a size proportionate to the aquarium. Sharks can be six inches long yet fully matured. But if you turn them loose in the ocean, they grow to their normal length of eight feet. That also happens to some Christians. I've seen some of the cutest little six-inch Christians who swim around in a little puddle. But if you put them into a larger arena – into the whole creation – only then can they become great."*

In fact, when Christians shrink from this larger arena, the world suffers from their absence. Until recent times, many believers have largely withdrawn from involvement in the affairs of the world, not wanting such things to taint them. They have retreated to the safety of their churches, seeing them as their field of Christian service. As a result, liberals and godless people have occupied the space left. This has especially affected those spheres of society that influence a nation's thoughts and behaviour, such as government, education, the arts and media. It is no surprise then that governments pass ungodly laws, while music, art, movies and magazines promote immoral behaviour, and learning institutions, especially universities, push secular humanism. This has been encouraged by the evangelical church's perception that transforming society was the cry of the liberal church and the true church should focus on saving souls.

German theologian Dietrich Bonhoeffer rather pointedly said, *"So long as Christ and the world are conceived as two opposing and mutually repellent spheres, man will be left in the following dilemma: he ...places himself in one or the other of the two spheres. He seeks Christ without the world, or he seeks the world without Christ. In either case he is deceived."* [11] Strong words; however, it is this very thinking that has led to the view that the world, and all that happens in it, is secular and corrupt, while the church, and all that happens in it, is sacred and godly. Thankfully, in the past few decades God has been correcting this short-sightedness and the church has been waking up to the Lord's command to position itself in all creation.

Look at the Big Picture

Some may argue that we find this problem of dualism mostly in the institutional church. Globally, Christians not connected to an organised church or denomination are a growing group. There is a shift taking place from the church as an organisation to the church as an organism, from the platform to the everyday arenas of life. Something less organised, and centred on all of life, is emerging. However, I do not believe that these emergent structures will supersede all previous ones. A range of church forms will always exist. God blesses the heart more than the structure.

Those involved in new expressions of church life may judge more traditional approaches as outdated. Yet God loves all structures if the heart and motive are pure. From house churches to mega-churches, institutional churches to unstructured groups, traditional churches to new churches, all can find a place in advancing the Kingdom of God. Believers should not fight over organisation and ideology and miss the big picture. Instead, we must discern the body of Christ – true believers are present in all structures – and trust the One who said, *"I will build my church"* to ultimately create a glorious church on the earth. This is not an excuse to tolerate formalism and dead religion. Rather, it is a call to unity and the need to work together to impact the world for Jesus.

Though we celebrate the widespread restoration of apostles, prophets, evangelists, pastors and teachers to the Body of Christ during the past fifty years, this has not been for elevating those leadership ministries to stardom. Rather, they have been restored *"to prepare God's people for works of service, so that the body of Christ may be built up, until we all reach unity in the faith and in the knowledge of the Son of God and become mature, attaining to the whole measure of the fullness of Christ."* [12] It is an error to limit these works of service only to the congregation; they are for all spheres of life. How many spiritual-gift analysis courses, for example, consign these gifts to the context of congregational ministry and service? The Body of Christ will not come to full maturity and unity until we see all of creation as our field of service, until leaders equip their people to minister successfully in that arena.

Now, I believe service in the church community is important. Paul wrote, *"So then, as we have opportunity, let us do good to all men, especially to those who are of the household of faith."* [13] Christians are part of a spiritual community and to use our gifts to serve within that community and help it grow is a priority. Moreover, we are to honour those who serve, especially leaders and those who teach the Word of God. We should be thankful for every person who contributes to church life either voluntarily or as paid staff.

However, it is a mistake for leaders to give the impression that the congregation is the exclusive field of worthy service. By doing so, they create a conflict within the people, causing a competition for their time. The church salted through society Monday to Saturday is as valid as the church gathered on Sunday. If leaders release their congregations into all fields of service by encouraging and validating the work they do, they will discover that people will willingly serve in the church community.

At the beginning of each year, my home church holds an anointing service where the leaders pray for all the members of the congregation and anoint them with oil. Senior pastor Luke Brough explains, *"At the start of each year we do not just commission our leaders, but we recognize that we are all members of the Body of Christ and therefore we all have a ministry to function in. Not everyone will pastor a church or preach on a regular basis like I do, but this does not mean their assignment is any less important than mine. In many ways our member's ministry role is more important as they are the body of Christ in the market place and their home. The eternal destiny of the people they are in contact with can be determined by their witness."* [14]

Worthy Work

"Work hard," said the apostle Paul to slaves, *"but not just to please your masters when they are watching. As slaves of Christ, do the will of God with all your heart. Work with enthusiasm, as though you were working for the Lord rather than people. Remember that the Lord will reward each one of us for the good we do, whether we are slaves or free."* [15] If this was written to slaves who had every reason to look down on the work they did, how much more should it apply to employees, parents, pastors, businesspeople, church workers, students, artists and the like? It is not merely the task we do, but rather how we do it, that gives it value. And if we see value in what we do, it will stimulate hope – hope that what we are doing is making a difference in the world.

Jane and I once had a meal with a car salesman friend and his wife. During dinner, I said to him, *"You know, selling cars for you is just as important as preaching messages for me."* He looked at me in disbelief. I knew exactly what he was thinking because I had once believed the same thing: an inspiring message can affect hundreds of lives and help people live well for God. How could selling used cars compare with that? Well, my friend is a Christian full of integrity. He sells good vehicles, which have been checked and repaired where necessary, and never charges more than the vehicle is worth. My friend has sold many vehicles over the years, and that translates into many satisfied customers who are driving safe, reliable vehicles. Now that is something of value in a world where car salesmen are often not trusted. In a dishonest world, honest people shine out and that causes others to wonder why. It's as the apostle Peter said, *"Be careful how you live among your unbelieving neighbours. Even if they accuse you of doing wrong, they will see your honourable behaviour, and they will believe and give glory to God on the day of visitation."* [16]

Like my friend, too many underrate the work they do, seeing it as both insignificant and ineffective compared to the more 'sacred' work of others. This robs them of the hope that their life and work matters – to God, themselves, and the cause of the Kingdom. My wife Jane battles with this. Trapped in a wheelchair, unable to do anything, she sometimes feels useless. Yet she is actually doing something of immense value: she radiates God in a difficult situation. And she does it beautifully, impacting so many lives. That, she has discovered, is her work at this present time. It has purpose and it gives hope to others in despairing circumstances. The person who discovers the true value of the work they do, no matter how tedious or insignificant it seems, is the person who will overflow with hope.

Notes
[1] Thomas Carlyle, Scottish essayist and historian (1795-1881)
[2] *The Purpose Driven Life*, Grand Rapids, Zondervan, 2002.
[3] 1 Corinthians 15:58

4 1 Corinthians 15

5 I am grateful to Alistair Mackenzie and his writings, as a source for this section on dualism. For more of Alistair's work, see the website www.faithatwork.co.nz.

6 Matthew 12:2

7 Matthew 12:10

8 Luke 3:22

9 John R. Schneider, *The Good of Affluence*, Grand Rapids, William B. Eerdmans Publishing Co., 2002, p.149.

10 One may ask then why Jesus commended Mary for doing an apparently devotional thing i.e. sitting at his feet as she listened to him teach, but did not commend Martha as she busied herself with manual tasks (see Luke 10:38-42). However, Jesus was not making a statement about the relative value of the two things; rather he was commenting on the importance of right priorities. Rather than enslaving us, all work must flow out of restedness, and the latter comes through intimacy with the Lord and taking time to rest in his presence.

11 *Ethics*, New York, Macmillan, 1975, pp.196-97.

12 Ephesians 4:12,13 (NIV)

13 Galatians 6:10 (RSV)

14 In the anointing service Pastor Brough calls the elders of the church forward, anoints them with oil and prays for a release of the blessing and power of God over them as they serve the Lord for the coming year. They in turn pray the same over the congregation. Many come forward as a couple, or family if the children are in the service. The children's church and youth church do the same. It has become a very special time in the life of the church.

15 Ephesians 6:6-8

16 1 Peter 2:12

Chapter Nine

Your Work Has Purpose

"Three grand essentials in this life are
Something to do,
Something to love,
And something to hope for." [1]

As we saw in the previous chapter, valuing the work we do is essential to stimulating hope. However, we only value work if we see its true purpose. Sadly, many think work is a curse. Just ask the harried homemaker or average employee on a Monday morning. Yet work existed before humanity sinned, because God worked when he created the world. He enjoyed his creative work and saw that it was good. His work reveals who he is and what he is like. The Bible says, *"For since the creation of the world, God's invisible qualities – his eternal power and divine nature – have been clearly seen, being understood from what has been made, so that men are without excuse."* [2]

Because God created humankind in his image, he gave them work to do – tending and ruling his creation. Moses writes, *"The Lord placed the man in the Garden of Eden to tend and care for it."* [3] God did not create work merely to provide for material needs, but to give a sense of dignity and purpose. Work in the Garden was pleasurable, fulfilling and very productive.

Imagine the scene. Adam and Eve, newly created, woke each morning to live another day in paradise. The sun always shone, the sky was always blue, and there were no storms, famine, drought or floods – just all year round perfection. [4] Tending the garden was a pleasure – there were no weeds, for everything was useful. Animals ate only vegetation, and there was nothing at all harmful in the garden. Adam and his wife could probably communicate in some way, even if only intuitively, with the animals (Eve was not at all surprised when the serpent spoke to her; much later, St. Francis of Assisi seemed to rediscover this ability). Created to live forever, Adam and Eve never aged. Everyday, God Almighty came into the garden and spoke with them face to face. Their work was to look after God's creation and know intimacy with him. What pleasure!

Enter Toil and Pain

After the fall into sin, when Adam and Eve rebelled against God, all this changed.[5] Paradise was lost. The earth fell under a curse. Work was with sweat; childbirth was with pain. Death and frustration entered creation. People became trapped in a cycle of working in order to live and living in order to work. Work was not the curse, but hard toil was. Instead of giving dignity and purpose, work became tiresome, and at times futile.

However, God had a plan to redeem this situation. Christ died to free us from the gulf of alienation from God and the curse of the toil and pain associated with work. In

Jesus, the work we do takes on new value. Now work does not save us from sin and separation from God – only faith in Christ does that. *"For it is by grace you have been saved through faith,"* said the apostle Paul, *"and this is not from yourselves, it is the gift of God – not because of works, so that no one can boast."* [6] Anything we do to try to earn God's forgiveness and acceptance is a dead work.

However, once we are saved, work can become purposeful, valuable, and joyful despite difficulties, and be rewarded both now and in the coming Kingdom. This is good work. Paul continued, *"For we are God's workmanship, created in Christ Jesus to do good works, which God prepared in advance for us to do."* [7] Good works are more than simply charitable acts. [8] They encompass all spheres of life and service, and include employment and vocation, education, prayer, studying the Bible, running a business, raising children, building a healthy marriage, daily chores, acts of kindness, caring for the environment, performing signs and wonders, congregational service and ministry, evangelism, art, music, sport, medicine, politics, worship – in fact anything God has called us to do that extends his Kingdom presence over all parts of creation.

It is not merely the works themselves, but how we do them that blesses others and lets God's light shine through us. God has prepared them in advance for us to do. That is why we need revelation concerning the things we do in life. Too many people travel down the wrong path and find frustration and disappointment. Ideally, when our work aligns with our natural and spiritual gifts and callings, there is productivity, joy and a sense of hope and purpose.

Even on the right path, toil and weariness still confront us, but in Christ, we can find the power to press through these barriers into productive work, which generates dignity, provision, service and the resources we need to be generous. Chuck Colson has said, *"Even in the harshest of* circumstances, work is still a gift of God that imparts a sense of personal fulfillment and useful service." [9]

Having walked the same path of toil as us, Jesus knows how to help us. The divine Son of God was tempted in his humanity in every way, except without sin. [10] This means he faced the same pressure to yield to the frustration and futility of work in a fallen world that we do. Isaiah the prophet said, *"But my work seems so useless! I have spent my strength for nothing and to no purpose at all. Yet I leave it in the Lord's hand; I will trust God for my reward."* [11] This is a Messianic verse. [12] Although spoken by the prophet, he is not talking about himself but the coming Messiah. Today, we see the success of what Jesus accomplished. Then, it was very different. Abandoned by many of his followers and surrounded by twelve wavering and fearful disciples, to whom he would leave the task of reaching the world with the Gospel, it appears that even Jesus felt frustration over the apparent lack of fruit in his ministry. However, he trusted his work and mission to his Father and left it in his hands. We must do the same.

A Gift from God

"What do people really get for all their hard work?" asked King Solomon, *"I have thought about this in connection with the various kinds of work God has given people to do. God has made everything beautiful in its own time. He has planted eternity in the human heart, but even so, people cannot see the whole scope of God's work from beginning to end. So I concluded that there is nothing better for people to be happy and to enjoy themselves as long as they can. And people should eat and drink and enjoy the fruits of their labour, for these are gifts from God."* [13] Solomon stated a timeless truth – to enjoy the fruit of our labour is a gift from God.

In the delightful movie, *"The Simple Life of Noah Dearborn,"* [14] Sidney Poitier plays a semi-rcluse, a man in his early nineties who actually looks decades younger. This is due, say the people of the rural town where Noah lives, to the enjoyment of his work. Relishing his uncomplicated lifestyle, Noah, a carpenter and builder, takes great pride in his work and has become a craftsman. In one scene, a developer offers to buy Noah's land, in order to build a shopping complex. Casting his sales pitch, the developer says:

"When's the last time you had a really good day?"

"Today," replies Noah politely.

Taken aback, the developer offers Noah cash for his land, but this is declined.

"Uh – think about all the time you'd have to relax and enjoy your life."

"My work is my life."

At that point the developer is beaten. As a boy, Noah learned a great secret from his uncle and mentor, who had told him, *"When a man loves his work, truly loves it, sickness and death will give up chasing you and finally leave you alone. Clear your mind of all that concerns you, and do the right thing with those hands God gave you."*

For many caught in the fast pace of modern living, where unhappy people work long hours to make money to find happiness, this is unimaginable. However, it is what Solomon was saying – to enjoy our work is a gift from God. Not only are we to enjoy work, but God also uses it to give us dignity.

Work Gives Dignity

Work should never be the measure of a person's value. If we use work to generate worth or to value who we are, we will become slaves to performance. Rather, the Father's unconditional love, as vividly demonstrated by Jesus dying on the cross for us, validates us as worthwhile. The Bible says, *"Because of Christ and our faith in him, we can now come fearlessly into God's presence, assured of his glad welcome."* [15] God has set his love on us. Through the blood of Christ in which we trust, we are recipients of that incredible love.

Possibly, you grew up in a home where affirmation came only when you accomplished something special – perhaps succeeding academically or doing well at sports. Maybe that has made you strive to please and perform, and you carry this over into your relationship with God. When I had cancer and became so ill with chemotherapy that I could do practically nothing, I discovered God still loved me. I felt his love and nearness more than in all the times I had laboured so zealously for him. This discovery began to liberate me from a lifetime of basing my self-worth on what I did. We do not work to earn his love; we work *because* he loves us.

Since the Father loves us, he gives us Kingdom work to do. Such Kingdom tasks dignify us, filling our lives with purpose. As God works in the world, so he calls us to share in the work he is doing: to tend and care for all his creation, and reveal him to a world that does not know him. What a privilege!

In Christ, we glimpse the new order. Through changed hearts and minds, we can overcome toils and trials and engage in useful, fruitful, and meaningful service and work. We labour by faith, because one day God will reveal the quality of each person's work.[16] In eternity, we will see the true worth of what we do. *"Blessed are those who die in the Lord from now on,"* wrote the apostle John, *"Yes, says the Spirit, they are blessed indeed, for they will rest from their toils and trials; for their good deeds follow them."* [17]

The very deeds we do will echo in the halls of eternity, determining our level of reward and responsibility in the new heaven and earth that God will create. This means the good work we do now has eternal value. Nothing we do here is too small if done with a right heart. Even a cup of cold water given in the Lord's name will not go without reward promised Jesus.[18] Thus, work generates hope, for our work in this present age will determine our reward in the age to come . Therefore, we are to value it.

"Most people, even professional people," writes theologian John R. Schneider, *"feel they are ultimately insignificant, that their work does not really matter in any ultimate way. At most they see their work as a means to an end, but not as something that is in itself good. The Parable [of the talents]...suggests that the real treasure of human history is hidden in ordinary people enlarging realms that hardly seem great...The message, I believe, is to enlarge and to dignify whatever realm God has given us. We should go about our work with royal pride and dignity."* [19]

Business pastor Martien Kelderman illustrates this with the following story, as told to him by a worker, who we will call Joe:

> "Joe was a railway maintenance worker. His hundred kilograms of muscle was part of a team that weeded and checked the tracks. They were responsible for a length of rail line. They would start at one end and work to the other end. When they got there, it was time to go back to the beginning and start all over again. The work was endless, boring and had all the hallmarks of futile activity. When challenged about changing jobs, Joe articulated a gospel of good work that went like this, 'No train will ever derail or crash and no one will ever be hurt on my watch. Furthermore, my mates and me, we do life together down there on the tracks. I know them better than their wives know them and they know me better. We

cry together and laugh together; we are loyal to each other. They know I am a Christian and they watch what that means forty hours a week.' Joe's care for safety, his excellence of work, and his people-keeping attitude will be part of the riches brought into the heavenly city by the saints. It is good work, it is the Lord's work and he is interested in it. Built on Christ, it will not be consumed."

The Bible says that in eternity, *"[The Bride] is permitted to wear the finest white linen. (Fine linen represents the good deeds done by the people of God.)"* [20] Amazingly, the good work we do on earth will form our clothing in the new world to come. Not just any good, but the good we do because of faith in Christ. The Bible likens good done without faith in Christ to filthy rags,[21] but good done in Christ becomes the finest white linen. Thus our good work inspires a glorious hope – we will literally worship before God's throne adorned in the good work we have done on earth! In the next chapter we will explore the link between work and worship further.

Notes

[1] Joseph Addison, English essayist, poet, and politician. (1672-1719)

[2] Romans 1:20 (NIV)

[3] Genesis 2:15

[4] See chapter eleven for an elaboration of conditions in the Garden of Eden.

[5] See Genesis 3:16-19

[6] Ephesians 2:8,9 (NIV)

[7] Ephesians 2:10 (NIV)

[8] In Ephesians 2:10 the Greek word used for work is 'ergon' which means toil (as an effort or occupation), an act, deed, doing, labour. (Strong's 2041)

[9] *How Now Shall We Live,* Wheaton, Tyndale House Publishing Inc., 1999, p.395

[10] Hebrews 4:15

[11] Isaiah 49:4

12 Isaiah 49:4 is a Messianic verse as it is linked to verse 6, which says, *"I will make you a light to the Gentiles, and you will bring my salvation to the ends of the earth."* Neither Isaiah nor Israel fulfilled this, only Jesus Christ.

13 Ecclesiastes 3:9-13

14 ©Trimark Pictures Incorporated, 1999.

15 Ephesians 3:12

16 See 1 Corinthians 3:13-15

17 Revelation 14:13

18 Matthew 10:42

19 *The Good of Affluence,* Grand Rapids, William B. Eerdmans Publishing Co., 2002, pp.191-192.

20 Revelation 19:8

21 See Isaiah 64:6

Chapter Ten

Your Work As Worship

"The most acceptable service of God
Is doing good to man." [1]

The band was in full flow, the worship leader was enthusiastic, the songs were inspiring – yet as I looked around at many in the congregation, they seemed strangely detached. This scene is not unusual amongst numbers of churches and Christian groups these days. In some places, worship is uplifting; the presence of God is real and the people actively participate. In others, it seems the people are passive and uninvolved in worship. Why is this? Is it the songs or the music style? Is it the worship leader or lack of devotion to God? Sometimes it is these but often the reason is more fundamental.

Speaking to a Samaritan woman, who argued with him about the correct place to worship, Jesus stated, *"Believe me, the time is coming when it will no longer matter whether you worship the Father here or in Jerusalem."* [2] In the age of the New Covenant, worship is no longer confined to certain places, times or ways. Jesus went on to say, *"But the time is coming and is already here when true worshippers will worship the Father in spirit and in truth. The Father is looking for anyone who will worship him that way."* [3]

The Father looks for true worshippers because they are not easy to find. To worship in spirit is to worship from the depth of our being, the essence of who we are and what we do. To worship in truth is to worship with sincerity and not pretence. The word worship itself comes from the Old English worthship[4], meaning worthy to adore. Jesus equated worship with a state of being, irrespective of place, while the Samaritan woman associated worship with a place. In the Western church, so influenced by dualism, we have focused on the place, the song, the music style and the worship leader. In so doing, we disconnect worship from ninety percent of our lives and confine it to thirty minutes on a Sunday. So then, what is the heart of true worship?

True Worship

"I appeal to you therefore brethren," said the apostle Paul, *"by the mercies of God, to present your bodies as a living sacrifice, holy and acceptable to God which is your spiritual worship."* [5] This verse pictures all of our lives offered to God as an act of worship, bending our will to his. Without sacrifice, there is no true worship. The cross of Jesus Christ was the ultimate act of worship. In some Bible translations, *'spiritual worship'* is translated *'reasonable service'*. [6] It seems these phrases are interchangeable. Worship and service are connected.

Some time ago, I planned a day of fasting, prayer, and study. I wanted to get close to God and enjoy intimacy with him. That morning, as I shaved, my mind started to wander; this is not uncommon when shaving, as it is an extremely mindless task. It was about my twelve thousandth shave, so I was on autopilot. As my thoughts drifted to the day ahead, I looked forward excitedly to spending time with God. Then I realised that I would first need to help Jane shower and get dressed, which would take about an hour and a half. Frustration swept over me. I wanted to get into the *'spiritual'* activity for the day, and helping my wife would hinder that. Then the Lord interrupted me. What He said would forever change the way I view worship.

"Your service to Jane is worship to me."

This astonished me – helping my wife was as meaningful and valuable to the Lord as fasting and prayer! This is no doubt what Jesus meant when he said, *"I assure you, when you did it to one of the least of my brothers and sisters, you were doing it to me."* [7] I related to Jane what had happened and apologised for thinking the way I had. Early in my caregiving role I saw, but all too often forgot, that my service to her was service to the Lord; now I understood that my service to her was also worship to him, and that is something I have never forgotten. It fills me with even greater hope that what I do for my wife is truly valuable work to God. Since then, I have seen work and worship as being intimately connected.

Work and Worship

Our work can be worship to God. When we see little value in what we do, it erodes dignity and encourages despair. When we see value in even the most menial task and offer it as worship to God, work and worship intertwine, and hope – the expectation that no act of reverence is worthless or will go unrewarded [8] – soars in our souls.

A Chinese pastor, Mingyen Chen, once visited our church and related how, when in a Communist prison, the authorities assigned him the most degrading work to break him. Day after day, he had to shovel out the sewage pits for the camp. It was a filthy, disgusting task, often necessitating his climbing into the pits to completely empty them. Yet he discovered that this was the only place in the camp that he could freely talk to God. No one else, including the guards, would come near him. It became the most precious place of intimacy and worship, his garden as he called it. He repeatedly sang, *"And he walks with me and he talks with me, and he tells me I am his own; and the joy we share as we tarry there no other has ever known."* He made a demoralising task a place of worship to God, and triumphed over the dark forces seeking to destroy him.

Thankfully, life does not throw many of us into such a place. However, the principle is still the same. As World Vision worker John Morrow has written, *"Our spiritual worship involves nothing less than offering up our everyday ordinary lives to God, so that all we think, say and do – our sleeping, eating, going to work and walking around life – is in sync with God's character and principles for holy, healthy living. The devoted parents and homemakers, the upright business person, the servant employee, the committed volunteer are worshipping God as much in their parenting, working and serving as in their times of intimate personal prayer or joyful corporate praise to God."* [9]

Community Worship

What value then does corporate or community worship have? It has great value. There is tremendous power in worship in unison. It is the pattern of heaven itself. [10] Corporate worship is a potent vehicle to arouse a sense of God's presence and power, stir the soul, and open the eyes and ears of the heart. It is special to gather with God's people, whether in a small group or large congregation, and to celebrate his goodness, worshipping in song and proclaiming stories of his work in our lives. However, if we disconnect worship from the rest of life, we will struggle in our corporate worship. The more we connect worship with our mundane, day-to-day lives, the more significant our corporate worship will become. Conversely, our worship together should inspire us to *"outbursts of love and good deeds"* [11] as we live in the world. It is not one or the other, but both.

I remember attending an extraordinary worship service a few years ago. Our church had received instruction on worship for the previous two Sunday evenings, and then devoted a third night exclusively to worship. Part way through the service, the glory of God – the weight and splendour of his presence – came into the meeting. At one point, a dozen or so women began to dance at the front of the church with great freedom and joy. Some 'dancing' I see in churches today makes me cringe, but what I saw that night was clearly choreographed by the Holy Spirit. At the same time, other people were on the floor crying out for God's mercy for their sins, while still others were on their feet praising God with all their might. The manifestation of his presence lasted for nearly two hours. That night, heaven kissed earth – and we all knew it.

At the end of the service a Korean lady, a recent convert to Christ, asked me, *"What was the silver cloud that moved across the platform and settled over the worship team?"*

"Did you see it in your mind?" I replied, thinking it was some kind of internal vision.

"No – I saw it with my eyes!"

Amazed, I explained that the Bible refers to 'the cloud of God's glory',[12] and she had glimpsed it. I have never been in a meeting like it before or since. Heaven opened for a few short hours and we bathed in it. Yet, I have learned that every day, the way I live, work and serve is an act of worship as precious to God as the worship I experienced that night. Too often, we confine God's presence to a meeting. Instead, we are to take that presence into the world around us, worshipping as we go, through the service we perform, the work we do and the way we live. Thus, there is a connection between our public worship in community and the worship we perform in the rest of our living.

The True Song

In his book *"Alabaster's Song"*, Max Lucado tells the story of an angel, Theodas, sent from heaven to earth to find a new song for the King of kings. Theodas had settled with a family for a few months and had grown friendly with their young son William. One day as they walked along, Theodas explained to William that God had created him to sing in the Lord's presence. Puzzled, William replied that he was not very good at singing.

"Not very good?" said Theodas, *"Why your singing is some of the most beautiful I have heard since I've been here. How can you speak such nonsense? Your song is the one I was sent here to listen to and take back to sing for the great King."*

"But I never sing!" protested William, *"Everyone makes fun of me when I do."*

"William, the song is not the sounds you make to music. The song is your life. You are the poem, the song, and the masterpiece!"

For Theodas, singing was something more than singing words. Songs, for him, could be moments of kindness or understanding or forgiveness. In fact, he heard a person's entire life as a kind of song. [13]

This story contains great insight into the breadth of worship. The song is our life and the things we do, offered to God. Here, we find meaning in even tedious tasks and difficult situations, and this gives us hope – confident expectation that our lives count for something and bring pleasure to God, who will one day reward us when everything that is hidden will be revealed.

Speaking of her work of caring for the sick and dying in India, Mother Teresa said, *"There is always the danger that we may just do the work for the sake of the work. This is where the respect and the love and the devotion come in – that we do it to God, to Christ, and that's why we try to do it as beautifully as possible."* [14] Mother Teresa understood more than most the connection between work and worship. Work offered to God as worship will be rewarded in the age to come.

That is our everyday hope!

Notes
1 Benjamin Franklin, US scientist, inventor, and statesman (1706 – 1790)
2 John 4:21
3 John 4:23
4 The actual word is 'weorthscipe' (Concise Oxford Dictionary)
5 Romans 12:1 (RSV)
6 'Reasonable service' is used in the NKJV and the Greek NT.
7 Matthew 25:40
8 Mark 9:41
9 Quoted at the funeral of his father, Peter Morrow, respected New Zealand apostle and prophet.
10 See Revelation 5:11,12 and 7:9
11 From Hebrews 10: 24, 25 which says, *"Think of ways to encourage one another to outbursts of love and good deeds. And let us not neglect to meet together, as some people do, but encourage and warn one another, especially now that the day of his coming back again is drawing near."*
12 See 2 Chronicles 5:13,14; Ezekiel 10:3,4; Matthew 17:5 for example.
13 *Alabaster's Song*, Nashville,Tommy Nelson (a division of Thomas Nelson Inc.), 1996, p.32

14 *The Missionary Position: Mother Teresa in Theory and Practice* by Christopher Hitchins, London, Verso, 1995, p.15.

PART THREE

ULTIMATE HOPE

"No eye has seen, no ear has heard, and no mind has imagined what God has prepared for those who love him," states the Bible. *"But we know these things because God has revealed them to us by his Spirit."* [1] We can know the things God has prepared for those who love him! Revealed by the Holy Spirit, they reach beyond this present life into the glorious world to come and are the ultimate reason for us to have hope.

Though a mystery hidden for long ages, God's plan has now been revealed to all creation. *"God has chosen to make known,"* said the apostle Paul, *"the glorious riches of this mystery, which is Christ in you, the hope of glory."* [2] When we turn from sin, turn to God, and have faith in Jesus Christ, he comes to live within us. This presence of Christ in our lives, and the coming of the Holy Spirit upon us, is the guarantee of what is coming in the future. It is the basis of all hope – it is the hope of glory. *"We have the Holy spirit within us,"* says the Bible, *"as a foretaste of future glory."* [3]

Hope for good things in this present life, though important, falls short of the principal reason for hope: God's unwavering commitment to heal a sin-ravaged world and restore it to a perfect, sinless state where there is no death, sorrow, sickness, war or lack of any sort. That is ultimate hope! All hope will find its final fulfillment in this future glory, when Jesus appears and the Kingdom of God will be finally and fully manifest on earth.

To understand this glory to come, we need to go back to the beginning. *"I write to you, fathers,"* said the apostle John, *"because you have known him who is from the beginning."* [4] We must understand what God began to do on earth when he made the first man and woman. When he created the Garden of Eden, God clearly demonstrated his original purposes for humanity. There, Adam and Eve enjoyed paradise and free access to the presence of God. God and humanity walked together as friends.

When, through Adam and Eve's rebellion, Eden ceased and the design of God became obscured, God later chose a temple to illustrate his plan. Providing a way back to the presence of God, it showed his desire to dwell again among his people. Today, that temple is a spiritual one: the church of the Lord Jesus Christ.

God's purposes began with a garden called Eden, and were resurrected in the temple. They will end with a city called the New Jerusalem. This glorious city, fashioned in heaven, and revealed upon a new earth in a future day, will see the completion of God's plan of restoration. From the garden to the temple to the city, God's purposes sweep panoramically through history. Paradise in the garden was lost. Paradise will be restored forever in the city, which will be the headquarters of a new heaven and earth.

Let's take a journey along this path. What was it like in the garden? What was God's purpose for mankind? What will it be like in the city? To understand the future and thus allow hope to reach its full power, we must look at the past, for God leaves signs along the highway of history, pointers of what is to come. Let's go back to the beginning...

Notes
1 1 Corinthians 2:9,10a
2 Colossians 1:27 (NIV)
3 Romans 8:23
4 1 John 2:13 (NIV)

Chapter Eleven

The Lost Garden

"This most beautiful system
Could only proceed from the dominion
Of an intelligent and powerful Being." [1]

Christmas Eve, 1968. For a brief moment, the earth's attention was directed away from its own problems, and towards three men orbiting another world. Apollo 8, the first manned mission to the moon in human history, had entered lunar orbit. As they circled the moon, NASA astronauts Frank Borman, Jim Lovell and William Anders witnessed a scene no human had ever seen. They watched as the earth rose over the moon's horizon, a blue and white orb hanging, beautiful yet fragile, in the yawning darkness of space. Its splendour left them awestruck. That evening, the crew gave a live television broadcast and, no doubt inspired by what they had seen, ended the broadcast by reading from the Bible. They took turns to read from the first chapter of Genesis, commencing with: *"In the beginning God created the heavens and the earth."*

In the beginning, God created. The idea of creation does not sit comfortably in a modern world that has committed itself and its philosophy of life to Darwin's theory of biological evolution. Believing that the universe probably started with an explosion of energy and matter (called the big bang) and that over countless eons, life evolved from simple molecules to the complex life forms found today, evolutionists maintain that living organisms are a product of random forces and natural selection. Claiming 'proof' from the fossil record, many scientists and learning institutions treat evolution as scientific fact when it is no more than a theory. It is a convenient belief for a world that does not want to be accountable to the God who made it. [2]

The Bible states, *"The fool says in his heart, 'There is no God.'"* [3] This is no doubt what the apostle Paul meant when he said, *"From the time the world was created, people have seen the earth and sky and all that God made. They can clearly see his invisible qualities – his eternal power and divine nature. So they have no excuse whatsoever for not knowing God. Yes, they knew God, but they wouldn't worship him as God or even give him thanks. And they began to think up foolish ideas of what God was like. The result was that their minds became dark and confused. Claiming to be wise, they became utter fools instead."* [4]

Amongst those who believe in a supernatural creation, there are three different views of beginnings. They are creation, intelligent design and theistic evolution. [5] Briefly, creationists believe in a six-day creation, Adam and Eve, a young earth (though a few creationists believe in an older earth, proposing a time gap between the creation of planet earth and the creation of life), the fall of man into sin, and the global flood of Noah's day. Creationists take the biblical book of Genesis, including chapters one to eleven, which deal with origins, as straightforward fact. Jesus said that those who did not believe the words of Moses (who wrote Genesis) would struggle to believe his words. Jesus spoke of Adam and Eve, and the flood in a literal sense, and did not consign them to myth. Creationists believe the fossil record supports the biblical view of a sudden creation. [6]

Today, a growing number of scientists, especially those who study cellular and stellar systems, question evolutionary theory. They and others hold to the theory of Intelligent Design. They claim life and the universe show evidence of complex design and thus there must be an intelligent designer. While a few speculate wildly that alien races from outer space may have seeded life on earth, most sensibly attribute that design to God, although they may or may not believe in the biblical account of creation.

Theistic evolutionists believe in evolution and that God initiated the process and sustains it. They treat Genesis as more allegorical than historical and thus not to be taken literally. Here, they are on slippery ground and this belief appears to be a convenient compromise to bridge the so-called gap between science and faith.

I am a creationist and write from that viewpoint. I have a science degree with honours in chemistry, love science, and believe the literal account of creation as found in the first chapters of Genesis. We should avoid fanciful ways of translating those scriptures; the simplest explanation is usually the correct one. There has been a satanic onslaught against Genesis in the past century or two. Satan knows that if people doubt the book of beginnings, they will also doubt Revelation, the book of endings. Revelation, the last book of the Bible, deals with hope. Thus, the devil, by destroying the message of Genesis, attempts to destroy human hope.

It is no problem for a supernatural God to create the earth in six days and start the human race with one couple. In fact, there is no need for science and biblical belief to be at odds. Thoughtful and honest scientists who study God's world will increasingly uphold the claims of God's Word. The Bible says that even inanimate things such as trees, fields, rocks and stars will praise God. More and more the earth and the universe around us will give up their secrets to careful and unbiased study and, literally, creation will speak, providing evidence for its Creator. As respected mathematics professor Wolfgang Smith has said, *"The physics of today is inviting at last the more thoughtful…to examine the 'question of God'."* [7] Those who have eyes to see will see.

So if in the beginning God created the world, what was the purpose of that creation?

The Purpose of Creation

God set a cosmic plan in motion when he made the heavens and the earth. He created them for a purpose and planned that the pinnacle of his Creation, humankind, would carry out that purpose. Father, Son and Holy Spirit said to one another, *"Let us make people in our image, to be like ourselves. They will be masters over all life – the fish in the sea, the birds in the sky, and all the livestock, wild animals, and small animals. So God created people in his own image; God patterned them after himself; male and female he created them. God blessed them and told them, 'Multiply and fill the earth and subdue it. Be masters over the fish and birds and all the animals.'"* [8]

His plan was that humankind would reproduce, fill the earth, rule it and steward its resources. To begin with, God placed the first man and woman in a manageable area called Eden. Now the whole earth was beautiful and lush, but Eden was special. The name Eden means delightful, paradise, and adornment. Eden was the jewel of the earth. The prophet Ezekiel called it the garden of God. [9] The greatest landscape designers on earth today would come nowhere near creating anything as beautiful as Eden. Here God put Adam and Eve to enjoy paradise and free access to the presence of God. They were also to tend the garden and cultivate it. Once they had excelled at that and increased their number, they were to go into the wider earth, to bring the order of Eden to it. Thus, when he created the Garden of Eden, God revealed his original purpose and design for humanity.

Eden was a microcosm of the larger thing God wanted to do in the earth. Adam and Eve were to prepare a place for God to come and live among them forever. This was always in the heart of God, as we shall see in the following chapters. He created humankind and gave them the earth as their domain. He then planned to bring his realm of Heaven to earth and to live with his people. What amazing grace, that God should come to his created creatures and be with them forever. However, Adam and Eve had to prove worthy of this.

Two Trees

At the centre of the garden, God placed two special trees. [10] The first was the Tree of Life. Apparently, the fruit of this tree could sustain an endless lifespan, for when God later ejected Adam and Eve from Eden, he did so because of his fear that they would continue to eat from the Tree of Life and live forever in a fallen state. [11] This is not as incredible as it may sound. Today, researchers are discovering the remarkable nutritional and medicinal properties of land and sea plants. When I had chemo-therapy to treat Hodgkin's disease in 1986, one of the drugs used was vincaleu-coblastine, or vinblastine for short. Extracted from the Madagascar periwinkle plant in the 1950's, vinblastine, along with two other drugs, has proven effective in causing remission in eighty percent of Hodgkin's type lymphatic cancers. Prior to this discovery, most Hodgkin's disease patients died from the disease. The periwinkle plant literally gave me life. How much more then the Tree of Life? Whatever it was, it had incredible power to sustain life.

The other tree at the centre of the garden was the tree of the knowledge of good and evil. Without its presence in the garden, choice did not exist. Forced love, which has no choices, is not love, but enslavement. Concerning these two trees one respected commentator says, *"The Tree of Life is associated with experiencing the life of God, including immortality. The tree of the knowledge of good and evil represents human autonomy, that is, self-rule and an assumed independence from God in all areas of life."* 12

God cautioned Adam and Eve not to eat its fruit or they would die. Sadly, they did not listen. How long they were in the garden before they rebelled against God is unknown. Possibly it was not very long, as they had no children at the time they sinned. Prior to this there had been rebellion in the ranks of the angels, God's other created order. Lucifer, one of the chief angels of heaven, was the most beautiful of all God's creatures, until the day he became proud. Not content with his place, he wanted to be like God. *"You were the perfection of wisdom and beauty,"* says the prophet Ezekiel. *"You were in Eden the garden of God."* 13 While some speculate Lucifer rebelled before the earth's creation, he was possibly in the Garden of Eden before he fell. Did he become jealous when God created other beings to bear more of God's image than he did? Angels were servants of heaven; humans were rulers of earth. Did he rebel after the creation of Adam and Eve, and then seek to corrupt God's newly created couple? It is possible. At any rate, as Satan, the adversary, he lied to Adam and Eve, telling them that they would not die if they ate from the tree. *"You will be like God,"* 14 he said, echoing his own evil ambition. Tragically, they believed his lie and sinned. Theologians call this act of rebellion the 'fall'; often we do not realise just how far we fell because we fail to appreciate how rich life was in Eden.

Just what were conditions like in the world before sin entered? Eden has long gone, but we can make some assumptions based on key verses in the early chapters of the book of Genesis.

They Saw God

Firstly, there was face-to-face intimacy with God. Adam and Eve were sinless and able to look upon God. In some embodied form, God walked in the garden each evening and spoke with them. [15] They talked with God in the same way you and I talk to friends. This is how God intended life to be. After they sinned, they hid from God when he came into the garden because they sensed their shame and guilt. This loss of intimacy was the greatest tragedy of the fall. Since that event, humanity has either been hiding from God or trying to find a way back through various dead-end paths. Only in Christ is there a way back. *"I am the way, the truth, and the life,"* said Jesus, *"no one can come to the Father except through Me."* [16]

No Death

Secondly, death did not exist. Diet was perfect, disease nonexistent. God created humanity to live forever. He said that they would die only if they ate the prohibited fruit. Otherwise, they would live forever. No wrinkles, lines, sags, or flab! The beauty industry would pay a fortune for a product that could do that. When Adam and Eve ate the forbidden fruit, they died, just as God had warned – not instantly, but by degrees. Adam died at 930 years of age (the Bible does not mention Eve's age at death but presumably she lived to a similar age.) The fifth chapter of Genesis records that the average life span from Eden to the time of the great flood many centuries later was 907 years (excluding Enoch whom God took alive to heaven at age 365).

There is no need to assume the years mentioned in Genesis were any shorter than years today. It is logical that beings created to live forever, despite the ravages of sin and the curse that came upon the world, would still live a very long time. Apparently, after his second coming, Christ will restore this longevity during his millennial or thousand-year reign on earth, presumably because of the near-paradise-like conditions that will attend his reign. [17]

After the flood, the lifespan fell to around 200 by the time Abraham was born a number of centuries later. Post-flood climactic changes possibly contributed to more rapid aging, but genetic changes affecting longevity are the more likely reason. In fact, God set a limit of 120 years on the human lifespan. [18]

Super Continent

Thirdly, there was one vast continental land mass. Moses records, *"And God said, 'Let the waters beneath the sky be gathered into one place so dry ground may appear.' And so it was.'"* [19] If the waters were in one place, then by implication so was the land. Even evolutionary scientists agree on this, citing a huge single continent that supposedly drifted apart over millions of years. Many creationists suggest, however, that the global flood of Noah's day broke up the land mass, wrenching the earth apart by the titanic forces unleashed at that time. A quick glance at a map of the world today will show that the major continents appear to be like parts of a giant jigsaw puzzle, which fit together with precision. The single land mass of the original creation would have aided the spread of humankind into all the earth.

Environmental Paradise

Fourthly, this great land mass was bursting with an abundance of food bearing plants and trees. [20] Adam, Eve, and all the animals were vegetarian. [21] There were no predators and prey. Humankind and God's creatures were at peace. Restoration of this harmony will occur in the millennial reign of Christ, when the wolf will lie down with the lamb, children will play with snakes, and the lion will eat straw like an ox. [22] God only permitted the eating of meat after the flood,[23] presumably because the flora alone could no longer sustain life.

The earth was a paradise with a variety and surfeit of food. No deserts spoiled it. No earthquakes shook it. No hurricanes ravaged it. No tsunamis flooded it. At the centre of it all, God planted the paradise of paradises – Eden. Here *"The Lord God planted all sorts of trees in the garden – beautiful trees that produced delicious fruit"* [24] A great river watered Eden. The name can also mean 'plain'. Thus, Eden probably contained a vast plain perfect for pasture and cultivation of crops. An ideal worldwide climate ensured many species grew much larger than they do today. Fossils show some flora and fauna were enormous in size when compared to today's equivalents. Some suggest that early humans may have been considerably bigger than people are today.

High Intelligence

Fifthly, God endowed Adam and Eve with brilliant minds. Genesis records, *"So the Lord God formed from the soil every kind of animal and bird. He brought them to Adam to see what he would call them, and Adam chose a name for each one. He gave names to all the livestock, birds, and wild animals."* [25] This incident illustrates the intellectual ability Adam had. He named thousands and thousands of species of animals and birds. Today, most of us struggle to come up with a few names for our children or pets! Moreover, with Adam and Eve's ability to talk directly with the Creator, they would quickly amass knowledge about the world from its designer.

Evolutionists believe that once-primitive humans have become more intelligent over time. The Bible hints that the opposite is true. There has been a dulling of intellectual capacity since the fall. While today there is an incredible increase and accumulation of knowledge and marvellous technological advance, we could have arrived at the same place much sooner if there had been no fall into sin and thus deterioration in intelligence. In addition, much knowledge would have been lost at the time of the epic flood. For example, the Bible records that Tubal-Cain, a pre-flood descendant of Adam's son Cain, was an iron craftsman. [26] Archaeological finds have shown that ironworking did not reappear until around 1500BC, some ten centuries after the flood.

Are rare geniuses like Einstein and others a glimpse of intelligence merely approaching what Adam and Eve had? Even today, experts puzzle over some of the engineering feats the ancients accomplished. Did they possess knowledge now lost or only being rediscovered? Did they also have access to supernatural powers which today we do not fully understand? If there had been no fall, humankind could perhaps have flown to the moon centuries ago, and may have reached the stars by now.

Yes, life in Eden was indeed paradise. The purpose of Adam and Eve was to multiply and take Eden to the rest of the earth, filling it with the knowledge of the glory of the Lord, to prepare it for God to come and dwell in his creation. All that was lost. The apostle Paul writes, *"Against its will, everything on earth was subjected to God's curse."* [27] Through Adam and Eve's disobedience, a curse came upon the earth

– the curse of toil in work, pain in giving birth, and death and decay. God sent Adam and Eve out of the Garden and barred their way back with mighty angels and a flaming sword. The flood would have finally destroyed all trace of Eden. There is no going back; environmentalists and utopians may try but will fail.

It grieved God to send Adam and Eve away. However, he had a plan to redeem them. The plan did not include a return to Eden; it involved moving forward to something better.

Notes

1 Sir Isaac Newton, English scientist and mathematician (1642 - 1727), speaking of the universe.
2 : See *Creation - Remarkable Evidence of God's Design* by Grant R. Jeffrey, Toronto, Frontier research Publications Inc., 2003 for an excellent discussion of the incredible complexity of life that debunks evolution and clearly points to design by a super-intelligent creator.
3 Psalms 53:1
4 Romans 1:20-22
5 For a detailed discussion of these three viewpoints and a critique of each, see the excellent book, *In the   Beginning: Three Views on Creation and Science* – available from Vision Network of New Zealand, PO Box 8082, Auckland 1035, New Zealand.
6 For answers to questions about Genesis and creation, see the website www.answersingenesis.org.
7 www.churchintoronto.org/Articles/Science%20&%20Faith/Science%201.htm
8 Genesis 1:26-28
9 Ezekiel 28:13
10 Genesis 2:9
11 Genesis 3:23
12 *Spirit Filled Life Bible*, Nashville, Thomas Nelson Publishers, 1991, p.7, footnotes on Genesis 2:9
13 Ezekiel 28:13
14 Genesis 3:5

15 Genesis 3:8

16 John 14:6

17 See Isaiah 65:20,22b. During the millennium, Christ will reign with resurrected believers over humans left alive at his return with his saints. These human survivors will worship him and multiply and fill the earth again. At the end of the millennium, they will be tested, and those who remain loyal will also receive resurrection bodies at the second resurrection and enter into the new heaven and earth, the rest being consigned to hell along with the disobedient of all history. See Revelation 20:5-15.

18 See Genesis 6:3. The threescore and ten often quoted in Psalm 90:10 (a psalm of Moses) was an observation of the Israelites' life spans in the forty-year wilderness wanderings, where God cut their lives short. One hundred and twenty is our potential lifespan, but poor diet and disease reduce this potential. Geneticists today confirm this, predicting that gene therapies along with disease prevention and proper diet will enable people to live longer, the figure of 120 often being cited. One geneticist, however, believes an age of 500 is attainable through genetic modification. In some parts of the world such as Okinawa, diet and lifestyle alone allow many to live to ages approaching 120.

19 Genesis 1:9

20 Genesis 1:11

21 Genesis 1;29,30

22 Isaiah 11: 6-8 and Isaiah 65:25

23 Genesis 9:3

24 Genesis 2:9

25 Genesis 2:19,20a

26 Genesis 4:22

27 Romans 8:20

Chapter Twelve

The Living Temple

*"One thing I have desired of the Lord,
that will I seek:*

*That I may dwell in the house of the Lord
all the days of my life,*

*To behold the beauty of the Lord
and to inquire in his temple."* [1]

Eden had perished, paradise was gone. However, humankind would eat from the tree of life again. *"For God so loved the world that he gave his only Son, so that everyone who believes in him will not perish but have eternal life."* [2] This remarkable statement broadcasts God's desire to restore everything lost in the fall. Yet, because of the rampant individualism in much of the world today, many reduce it to mean an experience of personal salvation. That is, if we turn from sin, believe that Jesus Christ died for us, and confess him as Lord, then we will have a life of purpose here on earth; and when we die, we will go to Heaven. As wonderful as this is, it is nowhere near the whole story. The bigger picture resounds with God's intent to restore creation to perfection.

This plan of restoration began before God created Adam and Eve. In making beings with free will, there was a risk that they would disobey their Creator. This was not a rigid predestination to sin; rather, the potential to do so accompanied the gift of free will. The potential to live in obedience to God was also there. Jesus proved this: in his humanity, he was tempted in every way but did not sin. [3] That the first man and woman sinned in a perfect world, however, shows people's tendency to choose wrongdoing. Foreseeing this before he created the world, God chose his Son to solve this very problem.

Before the foundation of the world, Christ, the Lamb of God, was slain. The Bible speaks of *"the Lamb of God who was killed before the world was made."* [4] While Jesus died on the cross at a finite moment in history, in eternity's timeless dimension, it was as if he had done so before time began. God's very act of creation was sacrificial – it cost him his Son's life.

The Plan Begins

From the moment of Adam and Eve's expulsion from the Garden, God set his plan in motion. Fallen humanity, however, did not cooperate. Aided by Satan's ongoing incitement to rebel against God, the world gradually became completely wicked. Saddened and provoked, the Lord determined to destroy all people, but found one man, Noah, who lived rightly. The Bible records that Noah *"consistently followed God's will and enjoyed a close relationship with him."* [5] He and seven other family members survived the great flood that deluged the whole earth and obliterated all people. God's plan survived with Noah.

When, centuries later, God chose Abraham, one of Noah's descendants, and promised to make him the father of multitudes, he furthered his plan of restoration. There would be a new race of men and women on earth who would obey God. Formed in slavery in Egypt and led into freedom by Moses, this new race was the nation of Israel.

On the journey from Egypt to the Promised Land of Canaan, God said to Moses, *"I want the people of Israel to build me a sacred residence where I can live among them."* 6 This sacred residence or tabernacle was a means whereby the Lord could live among his people. If they obeyed him, God promised Israel that he would, *"live among you and ... walk among you."* 7 Does this sound reminiscent of the Garden of Eden? This had been God's very intention when he created humankind to rule on earth, but the fall thwarted this. God could no longer live among a sinful people, lest the terrible fire of a holy God, unable to co-exist with sin, consume them.

After the Israelites carefully constructed the tabernacle or tent according to the design given to them, and offered burnt offerings and sacrifices on its altar, God filled it with his presence and glory. God lived among the Israelites, dwelling in a tent. Later, it would become a temple of stone during King Solomon's reign. Despite this, Israel continued to sin. Something more powerful than a temple of stone was required. Centuries later, it appeared.

"The Word became flesh," said the apostle John, *"and made his dwelling among us."* 8 Now God dwelt on earth in the form of his Son. Jesus himself claimed to be the temple of God. 9 When Jesus died on the cross, he bore the sin of the entire world from Adam and Eve to the end of time. The apostle Peter put it this way, *"Christ also suffered when he died for our sins once for all time. He never sinned, but he died for sinners that he might bring us safely home to God."* 10 Having accomplished this, he returned to Heaven. Yet God did not

leave the earth devoid of his presence. He created a new temple or dwelling place of God among people. No longer would God dwell in a temple of stone; he would now dwell in a temple of living stones.

A New Temple

With the Garden of Eden gone, God created a temple. While in Moses' day it was a tent of boards and animal skins, and in Solomon's day a temple of stone, today it is a spiritual temple. *"We are his house," said the apostle Paul, "built on the foundation of the apostles and the prophets. And the cornerstone is Christ Jesus himself. We who believe are carefully joined together, becoming a holy temple for the Lord. Through him you Gentiles are also joined together as part of this dwelling where God lives by his Spirit."*[11] *"God is building you,"* wrote the apostle Peter, *"as living stones into his spiritual temple."* [12]

Where does God reside on earth today? In his church, among his people. His people are those chosen from every nation and race, who believe that Jesus Christ is the Saviour of the world, and who have turned from their sins. Throughout the globe, no matter where the church of Jesus Christ is, there the dwelling place of God stands firm. The church is not merely buildings but people. Every believer is a temple of the Holy Spirit[13] and thus a bearer of God's presence in the world. Both the local and global church form a dwelling of God on earth. *"Don't you realise that all of you together are the temple of God,"* said Paul, *"and that the Spirit of God lives in (or among) you. God will bring ruin to anyone who ruins this temple. For God's temple is holy, and you Christians are that temple."* [14]

We lost the garden forever, but God created the temple as a temporary way of meeting humankind. That is what Christ's death is all about. God had incredible purposes for us originally. Now he has advanced a plan to restore those purposes – to gather humanity back to himself and dwell amongst us. In addition, the church is to extend God's Kingdom rule on earth[15], as Adam and Eve were to. Jesus told us to pray, *"May your Kingdom come soon. May your will be done here on earth just as it is in heaven."* [16] This will reach its completion when Jesus Christ returns. When the last living stone has been set in place, he will come.

Thus, we sell ourselves short if we think salvation is merely a matter of 'getting into Heaven.' We have so overemphasised heaven that we have lost sight of the central purpose of God: to bring Heaven to earth and fully manifest his Kingdom presence. This is why too many Christians live passive lives, uninvolved in the cause of the Kingdom. Why bother if we have a ticket to Heaven?

Heaven on Earth

Now, Heaven is an awesome place. Called variously Mount Zion, the City of the Living God, Paradise, and the New Jerusalem, it is the joyful gathering of multitudes of angels and the spirits of redeemed people who have died in faith and been made perfect. It is the home of God himself and of his Son, Jesus.

It is a place the apostle Paul found indescribable when God granted him a visit there. *"I was caught up into the third heaven,"* [18] Paul writes. *"Whether my body was there or just my spirit, I don't know; only God knows. But I do know that I was caught up into paradise and heard things so astounding that they cannot be told."* [19] Once, in a prayer meeting, I encountered the presence of God so powerfully that I could not stand, fell over, and for the next hour or so had a series of vivid visions. Though aware of what was happening around me, I seemed transported to a different realm. The visions culminated in seeing Jesus on a white horse leading the armies of heaven. He was so dazzling, and his eyes burned with fire, a fire of intense love for those who obey him, a fire of intense judgment for those who disobey him. This so awed me that I could not speak to anyone until the next day. What I saw was just a small glimpse compared to what Paul must have seen. No wonder he could not speak about it.

Heaven is an amazing and glorious place, but much teaching on the afterlife, though it stimulates hope, gives the impression that we will spend eternity with God in heaven. This is incorrect. God will spend eternity on earth with us! In fact, Heaven will come to earth. We have come from the Garden where God walked everyday and Adam and Eve saw him face to face. We are currently in the era of the temple, where he dwells with us by his Spirit and we glimpse him by faith. Yet, our destination is a city God has prepared in Heaven, which will one day come upon a new earth. *"For now we see in a mirror dimly,"* said the apostle Paul, speaking of the temple era, *"but then face to face."* [20] In the city era, God will complete his plan of restoration. Once again, he will live with us, we shall see him face to face, and rule with him over a new world.

Notes
1. Psalm 27:4 (NKJV)
2. John 3:16
3. Hebrews 4:15
4. Revelation 13:8. See also 1 Peter 1:18-20.
5. Genesis 6:9
6. Exodus 25:8
7. Leviticus 26:11,12
8. John 1:14a (NIV)
9. John 2:19-21
10. 1 Peter 3:18
11. Ephesians 2:20-22
12. 1 Peter 2:4
13. 1 Corinthians 6:19
14. 1 Corinthians 3:16

15 Kingdom Now teaching or Dominion Theology has become popular in recent years. This view asserts that the church will eventually rule the world and then hand it to a returning Jesus Christ. While I believe that a resurgent church of the last days will bring much Kingdom influence to the world – through the proclamation of the gospel, good works, signs and wonders, and by being salt and light in society – it will take the return of Christ to finally and fully usher in the Kingdom of God on earth.

16 Matthew 6:10

17 Hebrews 12:22-24

18 The first heaven is the sky, the second heaven space, and the third heaven the City of God.

19 2 Corinthians 12:2-4

20 1 Corinthians 13:12 (NKJV)

Chapter Thirteen

The Coming City

"It is for you that paradise is opened,
The tree of life is planted,
The age to come is prepared,
A city is built." [1]

Defying the law of gravity, it descended slowly from heaven, a massive, cubic city measuring over two thousand kilometres[2] on all sides, the base as large as two-thirds the land mass of Australia, the top reaching into space. Made of gold as transparent as glass, and with walls and foundations of precious stones, the city contained countless mansions, enough for every person of faith who has ever lived. [3] Its grandeur wasn't just material however. God's splendour and presence were the source of its unspeakable radiance. This was the most perfect thing ever seen by the human eye. On a new earth[4] without sea or ocean, the City of God, the New Jerusalem settled – headquarters of a new universe. Thus, the apostle John witnessed the completion of God's plan of restoration outworked over millennia since the fateful day that Adam and Eve lost Eden and the earth fell under a curse. In this amazing vision, the apostle saw more than the end of this present age; he saw the beginning of another. [5]

A Source of Hope

What John saw has proven a source of hope for all generations of believers, especially in times of adversity. Others have seen this city, too. Today, thanks to modern medical practice, many who have died and been resuscitated have claimed to have had out-of-body experiences. A number describe visiting heaven and seeing a city with various levels, streets of gold as clear as crystal, and many beautiful mansions, just as John described.

Listen to the account of one cardiac arrest victim:

"Immediately my spirit left my body, I saw the City of the Great King... I was looking down on the most dazzling sight imaginable. All the adjectives one could use – beautiful, splendid, picturesque, colourful, magnificent – are totally inadequate to describe this place...there were three levels in that city and seemingly millions of miles of streets; avenues of solid gold, not paved with gold but solid and yet at the same time transparent. It was the purest, cleanest, and brightest gold imaginable and looked like ribbons of magnifying glass. Everywhere, through the streets and as far as I could see, were millions of mansions." [6]

Compare John's description of the city: *"Then I saw a new heaven and a new earth, for the old heaven and the old earth had disappeared. And the sea was also gone. And I saw the holy city, the New Jerusalem, coming down from God out of heaven like a beautiful bride prepared for her husband. I heard a loud shout from the throne, saying, 'Look, the home of God is now among his people! He will live with them, and they will be his people. God himself will be with them. He will remove all of their sorrows, and there will be no more death or sorrow or crying or pain. For the old world and its evils are gone forever'"* 7 John goes onto say, *"The city was pure gold, as clear as glass."* 8

These words echo those given to Moses thousands of years before when God said, *"Build a tabernacle that I may dwell among them."* While the temple era partially fulfilled God's desire to dwell with his people on earth, the city consummates it. *"Look the home of God is now among his people. He will live with them."* Gone forever are the old world and its evils. The curse of pain, toil, death and decay that brought such sorrow has passed away; creation's groan has ended.

We will not spend eternity in a never-ending church service sitting on heavenly clouds with harps! This glorious heavenly city will come to earth, and God will live with his people. God will manifest his Kingdom – with its King present – fully and physically on earth. It is the ultimate act of a loving God, to bring his home, Heaven, to our home, earth, and for God and his people to be one forever. He will fully restore his presence, a presence lost in Eden, and only partially restored in the temple era. In fact, the city incorporates elements of both the garden and the temple.

The Temple Present

Like the holiest place where God dwelt in the temple of the Old Covenant, the city itself is a perfect cube. And its gates are always open. In other words, there is direct access to the presence of God. *"No temple could be seen in the city,"* writes John, *"for the Lord God Almighty and the Lamb are its temple. And the city has no need of sun or moon, for the glory of*

God illuminates the city, and the Lamb is its light." [9] Darkness never invades this city; the Lord bathes it in constant daylight. *"Its gates never close at the end of the day because there is no night"* [10] and *"the nations of the earth will walk in its light."* [11] This city is the Temple of God, so radiant with his presence, that it will light the new earth.

Eden Present

"And the angel showed me a pure river with the water of life, clear as crystal, flowing from the throne of God and of the Lamb, coursing down the centre of the main street. On each side of the river grew a tree of life, bearing twelve crops of fruit, with a fresh crop each month. The leaves were used for medicine to heal the nations. No longer will anything be cursed." [12]

As there was a great river in Eden, [13] so a mighty river also flows through the city. The main street is the heart and centre of any city and it is here that the river flows. Because its source is the throne of God, the river contains the crystal-clear water of life. Everything about the city is pure, clear, and transparent. On each bank grows a Tree of Life, nourished by the life-giving waters. Two Trees of Life! Twelve crops of fruit to bring healing and perpetual life. [14]

In Eden, there were also two special trees. One was the Tree of Life, the other the tree of the knowledge of good and evil. This latter tree, through which death came, is absent in the city. The Lamb has forever paid for evil and broken the power of the sin nature in humanity. Only the knowledge of good remains. In their resurrection bodies, the saints are like Christ, and never again will there be any potential to sin. In place of what proved to be a tree of death, there is a second tree of life. The curse of sin and death is completely broken!

No doubt the wider, oceanless earth outside the city will be at least as luxuriant and beautiful as Eden was. If God's first creation was very good, then his new creation will be even more glorious. John mentions nations and kings bringing their glory into the city. This could refer to the nations and rulers of the old earth, but it is conceivable that nations of redeemed, glorified people will inhabit the new earth, with the city as their temple, home, and central government. With the whole earth a single, huge, border-less landmass, there will be no geographic isolation. This is very different to many people's concept of eternity!

The Ultimate

I believe that technology, art, music and many other facets of creation will be present in the new earth. God will not return us to some primitive, agrarian state. He has placed secrets in his creation that will unfold to us as never before. There will be both work and worship. *"For the throne of God and of the Lamb will be there, and his servants will worship him."* [15] Servants mean there will be service. Those permitted to be part of the new world, who have believed in the Son, will both serve God with purposeful tasks in eternity and worship him with adoration, for *"they will see his face, and his name will be written on their foreheads."* [16]

That is the ultimate wonder of the city: seeing God's face. *"Now we see but a poor reflection as in a mirror,"* wrote the apostle Paul, *"then we shall see face to face."* [17] Face to face. It is the privilege Adam and Eve had but then lost. It has been the longing of God's people throughout history. King David distilled this hope when he sang, *"I will see you. When I awake, I will be fully satisfied, for I will see you face to face."* [18] In one of the oldest and clearest statements on the resurrection in the Bible, Job looked beyond his intense suffering and prophesied, *"I know that my Redeemer lives, and that he will stand upon the earth at last. And after my body has decayed, yet in my body I will see God! I will see him for myself. Yes, I will see him with my own eyes. I am overwhelmed at the thought!"* [19]

We should be overwhelmed too. Overwhelmed that Jesus made it possible – that on the cross he shed his blood for our sin! If he had not, then the City of God would remain in Heaven, forever beyond the reach of men and women. *"For you know that God paid a ransom to save you from the empty way of life inherited from your ancestors,"* marvelled the apostle Peter, *"and the ransom he paid was not mere gold or silver. He paid for you with the precious blood of Christ, the sinless, spotless Lamb of God. God chose him for this purpose long before the world began, but now in these final days, he was sent to earth for all to see. And he did this for you."* [20] What gratitude this should inspire in us! What a privilege to tell others about this wonderful 'Good News.' Every time I see someone give his or her life to Christ and receive God's forgiveness, it moves me. This truly is amazing grace. *"The sin of this one man, Adam, caused death to rule over us,"* said the apostle Paul, *"but all who receive God's wonderful, gracious gift of righteousness will live in triumph over sin and death through this one man, Jesus Christ."* [21]

The Second Adam and Eve

Jesus not only died to bring us to the Father; he also died to bring the Father to us. In the new earth, Christ will present the church to the Father. Likewise, the Father will present the church to the Son for his Bride. We will be forever married to Christ, the Lamb of God. The city of redeemed people made perfect is, said John, *"the bride, the wife of the Lamb."* [22] This speaks of love. The city will be our home. This is why Jesus said there would be no marriage between people in the resurrection. [23] There is only one marriage in the new heaven and earth – the Bride of Christ married forever to Jesus.

Think of it: Christ, the second Adam, [24] will stand with his bride, the second Eve, in a new creation! What the first Adam and Eve failed to do in ruling the earth in righteousness, the second Adam and Eve will achieve. *"The end of God's ways,"* said German pietist Freidrich Oetinger, *"is loveliness."* [25] Who knows what purposes will unfold as Christ and his Bride rule a new universe for eternity, under the Father's approving smile? That is worth living for and holding on in faith to receive. That is better than the temporary pleasures of sin or whatever else this world has to offer.

"We are looking forward to the new heavens and new earth he has promised," said the apostle Peter, *"a world where everyone is right with God."* [26] God has revealed these things not to create escapists who fantasise about a future world while cruising to eternity, but people who live with purpose and unshakable hope in this life, no matter how mundane or difficult that life appears to be. Let me illustrate this with the following story.

A Cathedral Burns

In 1666, fire engulfed the greater part of the city of London. One of the buildings destroyed was old St. Paul's cathedral, a wooden structure quickly swallowed up by the flames. The church authorities decided to build a new stone cathedral, grander than the first. They commissioned Christopher Wren, renowned architect of his day, to design it. After they rejected a number of designs as being too radical, the bishops finally chose the design that today is St Paul's Cathedral in London. Building commenced in 1675 and took thirty-five years to complete.

The story is told that early in the construction, some wealthy gentlemen in fine clothing came onto the building site. Looking around, they noticed two men hard at work excavating a deep trench, which was probably one of the footings for the foundation of the cathedral. Intent on their work, the two workers, did not notice the men observing them. Finally, the gentlemen wandered over to the trench, peered in, and asked, *"Excuse me men, what are you doing?"* Putting down his shovel with a grunt of irritation, the first man replied tersely, *"I'm digging a trench."* The second worker looked up and with a beaming face said, *"I'm building a Cathedral for Christopher Wren!"*

Two men in a trench, doing the same work, yet both had entirely different attitudes! One saw only the trench. The other saw the finished cathedral and was thrilled to be part of its construction. Perhaps he had glimpsed the architect's plans or imagined what the finished structure might look like.

Life and work is like that. Every day of the week, you and I are in the trench of life doing mostly routine, ordinary things. At times, we may feel like the first worker. Heads down in the trench, all we see is the dirt that is a hindrance to getting the task finished. Or, we can be like the second worker who, holding the finished design in his mind and motivated by the hope it produced, saw every shovel-load of soil as a stepping-stone to completing the task. When we see God's glorious plan for the world, when we see the big picture, then what we are doing in life will take on a greater sense of purpose.

Just like the visionary man in the trench helping to build the cathedral, the City of God should inspire us to see that what we do now contributes to its building. Only then does the trench of life make sense. *"By his grace there is eternal glory buried within the passing smallness of our lives,"* writes John R. Schneider. *"And the parable [of the talents] leads us to trust that what we do in the small matters...provided we do it in keeping with faith in the King, reaches in some indescribable way into eternity, and gives shape to the homes and dominion we will have in the age to come."* 27

As we have learned, hope is a confident expectation of future good. It reaches into eternity and glimpses what is to come. *"If we have hope in Christ only for this life,"* said Paul, *"we are the most miserable people in the world."* 28 It is fine to have hopes and dreams for this life, but if they end there, what good is that? Hope for physical healing alone is not what has sustained Jane or me in our battles with sickness. Rather, it is also the hope of what is to come – reigning with Christ in a new heaven and earth where there will be no sickness or sin or poverty or war or death – a hope that reaches into eternity, beyond this life, beyond the grave. It is the hope of a world restored to God, the Kingdom of God fully manifest in all its glory, and of the resurrection of the dead. This is the hope of glory – our ultimate hope.

We are pilgrims on a journey from a garden to a city, children of Abraham, the pilgrim father of faith. He was content to live in a tent all his life. *"Abraham did this,"* says the book of Hebrews, *"because he was looking forward to a city with eternal foundations, a city designed and built by God."* 29 When we too glimpse the City of God, the completion of God's plan of the ages, it will change the way we live. The apostle Paul saw it and declared, *"I run straight to the goal, with purpose in every step."* 30 Paul journeyed well to the finish line, and so should we.

Notes

1 From the first-century Jewish apocryphal writing 2 Esdras 8:52 (abbreviated).

2 Actually 2220 kilometers or 12000 stadia (12 X 1000). Some see these dimensions as symbolic of perfection, completion and government. Nothing prevents the dimensions from being exact, however, and this is more likely. However interpreted, the city is huge.

3 Revelation 21&22 and John 14:2.

4 There is some debate as to whether the new earth will be a completely new creation or a recreation of the old earth. 2 Peter 3:10 says, *"But the day of the Lord will come as unexpectedly as a thief. Then the heavens will pass away with a terrible noise, and everything in them will disappear with fire, and the earth and everything on it will be exposed to judgment* (laid bare).*"* Some see the fire as purifying the old earth, which will be re-established. However, Peter speaks of this event in the next verse as *"the day when God will set the heavens on fire and the elements will melt away in the flames."* That the elements (the basic building blocks of all matter) melt seems to point to a total destruction of the old and the creation of a brand new earth and heavens.

5 A thousand years before, Christ returns to earth to defeat a worldwide rebellion against God's rule. Evil will have reached its peak as in the days of Noah, and God will act. Just prior to this, Christ will raise dead believers (and change living ones) and snatch the church – a church swollen by the unprecedented preaching of the gospel and a worldwide evangelistic harvest – off the earth, an event popularly called the Rapture (see 1 Thessalonians 4:16,17). At that time, believers receive new resurrection bodies that will be immortal, glorious, powerful, and spiritual (controlled by the spirit and not the flesh). Christ then returns to judge and rule the nations for a thousand years, a period called the Millennium. (This assumes a pre-millennial return of Christ. For other possible scenarios of his return, including Rapture and tribulation theories, see *The Spirit Filled Life Bible*, Nashville, Thomas Nelson Publishers, 1991, pp 1948-51.)

The Millennium will be a time of paradise on earth and will see the fullest manifestation of God's kingdom since Eden. The resurrected believers will rule with Christ over surviving humankind, who will multiply and enjoy long lives under such benign rule. During this time, God imprisons Satan and the earth enjoys prosperity, peace, provision and harmony. The knowledge of the glory of the Lord will fill the earth. See Revelation 20:1-6, Isaiah 2:2-4; 11:6-10; 65:20-25.

When the thousand years end, God will loose Satan for a short time as a final test of humanity. As before, the serpent uses his age-old lies to convince people that they would be better off ruling themselves. Many will be deceived and seek to overthrow

Christ and the resurrected believers. It will be futile resistance however. The rebels will be defeated, judged (together with the wicked of all ages) and cast into hell forever, along with the devil (see Revelation 20:7-15). Then God will create new heavens and a new earth that welcomes the City of God upon it.

6 *The Final Frontier* by Richard Kent&Val Fotherby, London, Marshall Pickering, 1997, p.71.

7 Revelation 21:1-4

8 Revelation 21:18

9 Revelation 21:22-23

10 Revelation 21:25

11 Revelation 21:24a

12 Revelation 22:1-3a

13 See Genesis 2:10

14 This is similar to the prophet Ezekiel's vision in Ezekiel 47:1-12 in which he describes a river flowing from a newly built temple (almost certainly of the Millennium era) through the desert of Jordan to the Dead Sea, where it will make the salty waters pure. All kinds of fruit trees will grow along its banks, bringing life and healing. The tree of life, one on each side of the river in the New Jerusalem, is, however, reserved for that city.

15 Revelation 22:3b

16 Revelation 22:4

17 1 Corinthians 13:12 (NIV)

18 Psalm 17:15

19 Job 19:25-27

20 1 Peter 1:18-20

21 Romans 5:17

22 Revelation 21:9

23 Matthew 22:30

24 1 Corinthians 15:45

25 Freidrich Oetinger (1702-1782)

26 2 Peter 3:13

27 *The Good of Affluence*, Grand Rapids, William B. Eerdmans Publishing Company, 2002, p.192, commenting on the parable of the talents in Luke 19:11-27.

28 1 Corinthians 15:19

29 Hebrews 11:10

30 1 Corinthians 9:26a

Chapter Fourteen

Reaching the Finish Line

"The future is purchased,
By the present." [1]

Seabiscuit. This horse with the strange name captivated a Depression-wracked America in the 1930's. Perceived somewhat inaccurately as an underdog (he had won a number of races before coming to greater fame with a new owner and trainer), Seabiscuit won the hearts of the afflicted masses. He was an ungainly looking animal, smaller than most other racehorses, with misshapen knees. Most sports commentators wrote him off, however, he proved them wrong. Mostly ridden by a half-blind prize-fighter turned jockey by the name of 'Red' Pollard, Seabiscuit went on to triumph over a number of famous racehorses of his day.

One race in 1938 captured the nation's imagination more than any other had because it pitted Seabiscuit against War Admiral, a thoroughbred from the East. Big, strong, and muscular, War Admiral looked every inch a champion. Crowds thronged to watch the race, and a nation stood still to listen in by radio. Neck and neck, the two horses raced, until the home straight when Seabiscuit left War Admiral standing, and won by a handsome four lengths. Red Pollard (who did not ride in the race due to injury) later quipped, *"Seabiscuit... made a rear admiral out of War Admiral!"* The crowds went wild; Seabiscuit became a legend. The nation loved him. He gave hope to the little man, the underdog, the despairing, that they too could realise their potential, something hard to believe in a nation pained by the Great Depression. Seabiscuit represented hope – the hope that ordinary souls could become champions.

We too can identify with this little horse that accomplished gigantic feats. Though we appear ungainly because of the effects of humanity's fall into sin, through Christ, we find ourselves under new ownership and there is a champion in each of us. God sees it and so must we. Like Seabiscuit, we are in a race to win a prize. *"You also must run in such a way that you will win,"* said the apostle Paul. *"All athletes practise strict self-control. They do it to win a prize that will fade away, but we do it for an eternal prize."* [2] Our eternal prize is the City of God.

From the garden to the temple to the city, God's purposes sweep panoramically through history towards the glorious state of that golden metropolis. Those purposes began with a garden called Eden, and were resurrected in the temple; they will end with a city called the New Jerusalem. Paradise was lost forever in the garden, but will be restored forever in the city. It is our final destination, our ultimate hope and prize and should completely revolutionise the manner in which we live, and view the church.

The church is more than a local congregation. She is the Body of Christ, the temple of living stones, comprising believers on earth and in heaven. She is the instrument to extend the Kingdom of God, and the Bride of the Lamb destined to become co-regent over a new earth and heavens.

When Christians become embroiled in debates over structure, beliefs, music, leadership style and other peripheral matters, they are being short-sighted. We must see what God is building. The entire Bible is the history of God building a dwelling place so that he could come and live among his people. Jesus meant it when he said, *"I will build my church."* He also added, *"All the powers of hell will not conquer it."* [3]

Absolute Triumph

The apostle Paul, speaking of the resurrection and the age to come, wrote, *"There is an order to this resurrection: Christ was raised first; then when Christ comes back, all his people will be raised. After that the end will come, when he will turn the Kingdom over to God the Father, having put down all enemies of every kind. For Christ must reign until he humbles all his enemies beneath his feet. And the last enemy to be destroyed is death. Then, when he has conquered all things, the Son will present himself to God, so that God, who gave his Son authority over all things, will be utterly supreme over everything everywhere."* [4]

This truth gives such great hope! The Devil and all his demons will one day be beneath Jesus' feet. Sickness, death, rebellion, poverty, and war will be under his heels. When he has done that, he will come to his Father and say, *"It is all for you."* Then God will be utterly supreme over everything, everywhere. This is where God is taking us. Our broken world – far removed from the original creation – hardly resembles this presently. However, the Kingdom of God has invaded the planet. John the Baptist announced it, Jesus demonstrated it, and the Holy Spirit shows us the fullness yet to come. It is both present and future. There is an age to come, but first there is an age to be won.

This age will be won by people of hope who realise that every act of reconciliation now points to the day when there will be total love in relationships, every healing or deliverance to the day when there will be no more sickness or demons, and every act of generosity to the day when there will be total provision and no poverty. These acts herald God's incredible plan for restoration, and his zeal to restore all that humanity lost in Eden. Far from reducing us to inactivity, that plan should inspire passionate involvement in advancing God's Kingdom and doing his work, one good deed at a time.

Therefore

"Therefore, my beloved brethren," said Paul, *"be steadfast, immovable, always abounding in the work of the Lord, knowing that in the Lord your labour is not in vain."*[5] This is the last verse of First Corinthians chapter fifteen, a chapter that declares the resurrection and ultimate triumph of Jesus over all things. Consequently, we are not to have an escapist mentality, merely wanting to coast to heaven; but we are to live responsibly here and now. We should see all of life as our field of work. What we do here will have reward there. God will waste nothing we do in this life, if done for him.

"Without wavering, let us hold tightly to the hope we say we have, for God can be trusted to keep his promise," says the Bible. *"Think of ways to encourage one another to outbursts of love and good deeds...especially now that the day of his coming back again is drawing near."* [6] Instead of inspiring careless living, hope in his coming should lead to eruptions of love and good deeds. A number of commentators today believe that the church is undergoing a reformation as significant as the Protestant reformation of Luther's day. That was a reformation of creed; today there is a reformation of deed – faith

expressed in practical actions of love and supernatural power. This will powerfully attract an increasingly problem-laden, hope-deprived world, which will become inquisitive. *"Always be prepared,"* said the apostle Peter, *"to give an answer to everyone who asks you to give a reason for the hope you have."* [7]

With wars, terrorism, natural disasters and the breakdown of moral order shaking the world today, believers must anchor their hope in God and the understanding of his times and seasons. If, in the midst of these violent global shakings, we perceive the work he is doing, then hope will remain, and we will be beacons for others. *"For He [Jesus] must remain in heaven until the final restoration of all things,"* preached the apostle Peter. [8] Within his grand scheme of restoration, there are times in history when the Holy Spirit emphasises certain biblical truths to help the church better align with the overall purposes of God. If we are to journey well and avoid careless living, we must recognise these seasons. Although the Spirit of God is emphasising a number of things today, I believe there are two that are high on his list: that God will fill everything everywhere with the presence of Christ, and that everyone everywhere will hear the Gospel.

Everything, Everywhere

The Bible says, *"The church is his body; it is filled by Christ, who fills everything, everywhere with his presence."*[9] God desires to fill everything everywhere with the presence of his Son. Now there are three aspects to the presence of God:

- ✎ Firstly, there is God's invisible presence or omnipresence – his presence fills the universe and is all around us.

- Secondly, there is his future, visible presence – when Christ returns to rule the earth, the whole world will see him come in power, and bow to him.

- Thirdly, there is his manifest presence now – his invisible presence becoming visible. This occurs when God moves supernaturally: he heals the sick, works miracles, or makes his presence felt in some tangible way. As well, his manifest presence includes his presence as it shines through his people.

As an example of this third aspect, the technical team in my previous church wanted to minister not only within the church community, but also within the community at large. They adopted a school and offered to help with the lighting and sound for its annual musical production. They faithfully did this for a number of years, earning the heart-felt thanks of teachers and pupils alike. Through this good-will, one of the youth pastors became a chaplain to the school. Not only did he counsel many of the students, but he also had an impact on the teaching staff. As a result, the deputy principal gave his life to Christ. These people brought the presence of Christ into that school.

Everyone, Everywhere

Jesus said, *"Go into all the world and preach the good news to everyone, everywhere."* [10] If Christ's presence is increasingly to fill everything everywhere, then everyone everywhere is to hear the Gospel. Presence and proclamation. Presence without proclamation may produce a good deal of light but a small harvest. Conversely, proclamation without presence may produce a bigger harvest but little permanent change in society. God wants church to return to the strategy shown to the apostle Paul. *"I have brought the Gentiles to God,"* he revealed, *"by my message and by the way I lived before them. I have won them over by the miracles done through me as signs from God – all by the power of God's Spirit. In this way I have fully presented the Good News of Christ."* [11]

Some time ago, during a Sunday worship service, I saw in my mind a picture of an elderly man with a question mark over his head. I sensed his name was Jim. At the end of the singing, I explained what I had seen. A young woman responded saying that her grandfather Jim was seriously ill in hospital. I told her that I believed he was asking questions, time was short for him, and that she should go and talk to him. The next day she went. The woman's grandmother said that Jim, who had never had any time for God in his life, had started asking questions about God. The young woman led her grandfather to Christ. A short time later, Jim died. Everyone, everywhere. The Lord does not want any to perish. I noted that the Holy Spirit initiated all this in a worship service and literally moved God's presence from that service into a hospital room, saving a dying man. He is serious about us engaging with his creation. As we journey towards the City of God, the work and service we perform in the world can make a powerful difference for good.

Finishing the Journey

What then does it mean to journey well? It means to keep the prize in view, travel through life bringing the presence of Christ into our world, and to make known to everyone, as God grants the opportunities, the reason for the hope within us. *"Let us not become weary in doing good,"* encouraged the apostle Paul, *"for at the proper time we will reap if we do not give up. Therefore, as we have opportunity, let* us do good to all people, especially those who belong to the family of believers." 12 To journey well means to cross life's finish line, spurred on by the cheering inhabitants of the City of God, and stand before the Lord, not with shame or apology, but with the joy that we have lived the best possible life with the resources he gave us. It is to enter that glorious city, from which we will one day reign over a new heaven and earth. That is God's dream for our lives, and his dream should become our dream. *"And now,"* said the apostle Jude, *"all glory to God, who is able to keep you from stumbling, and who will bring you into his glorious presence innocent of sin and with great joy!"* 13

Journey well now! Endure hardship now! Never doubt God's goodness, become embittered, and lose hope. *"That is why we never give up,"* explained Paul. *"Though our bodies are dying, our spirits are being renewed every day. For our present troubles are quite small and won't last very long. Yet they produce for us an immeasurably great glory that will last forever! So we don't look at the troubles we can see right now; rather we look forward to what we have not yet seen. For the troubles we see will soon be over, but the joys to come will last forever."* 14

That is our ultimate hope!

Notes

1 Samuel Johnson, English poet, essayist, and journalist, 1709-1784.
2 1 Corinthians 9:24b,25
3 Matthew 16:18
4 1 Corinthians 15:23-26,28
5 1 Corinthians 15:58 (RSV)
6 Hebrews 10:23,24, 25c
7 1 Peter 3:15 (NIV)
8 Acts 3:21
9 Ephesians 1:23
10 Mark 16:15
11 Romans 15:18,19
12 Galatians 6:9,10 (NIV)

13 Jude 24
14 2 Corinthians 4:16-18

Chapter Fifteen

Stay in Hope

"All the great things are simple,
And many can be expressed in a single word:
Freedom; justice; honour; duty; mercy; hope." [1]

Hope, we have discovered, is one of the most powerful forces in the world for sustaining life and accomplishing good. It is the spring from which faith and love flow. Suffering, rather than quenching hope, actually strengthens it, if responded to in the correct way. Adversity, far from being a hope destroyer, is one of God's tools to multiply hope within our lives. God's promise to 'make the valley of trouble into a gateway of hope' remains powerful proof of this.

We have also seen that the work, play, worship and service in which we actively engage, not only carry the potential to advance God's Kingdom in this life, but also to gain reward in the world to come. Our work and hope are thus deeply interwoven. Ultimately, all hope reaches its pinnacle in the expectation of Christ's return to usher in the fullness of his Kingdom reign upon the earth, and the creation of a new world in which paradise is restored. In a world of increasing terror and pain, that is really good news.

I would have liked a Hollywood ending to this book, to report that God had visited my wife with healing, and rewarded our long held hope. However, life sometimes does not have a Hollywood ending – at least not yet. Jane and I still wait expectantly for God to fulfill his promise to us, and in the meantime have found a gateway of hope in our valley of pain and difficulty – a gateway that has opened into a widening path of service to God and mounting confidence in his incredible goodness. Our encouragement to other valley-travellers – we all encounter such valleys sooner or later – is to take heart from the words of Jeremiah the prophet: *"Blessed are those who trust in the Lord and have made the Lord their hope and confidence. They are like trees planted along a riverbank, with roots that reach deep in the water. Such trees are not bothered by the heat or worried by the long months of drought. Their leaves stay green, and go right on producing delicious fruit."* [2] Blessed are those who have made the Lord their hope.

And blessed are those who persevere and do not give up. *"Slowly, steadily, surely,"* declared the prophet Habakkuk, *"the time approaches when the vision will be fulfilled. If it seems slow, wait patiently, for it will surely take place. It will not be delayed."* [3] Slowly – steadily – surely. Most dreams and prophetic promises will go through this progression. Sadly, too many become discouraged at the slowly phase and give up. However, if we will add our steadily to life's slowly, then there will be God's surely. This equation is valid for all the promises and dreams God has given us: slowly plus steadily equals surely. And that equals great hope.

At a conference I attended once, Bill Hybels, pastor of Willow Creek Community Church in Chicago, Illinois, encouraged delegates to never lose hope: *"Lost people can still be found and sick people can still be healed. The world is asking today, 'Is this how it will all end? Is there no hope? Will war,* poverty, and violence increase and keep on increasing?'" Hybels emphatically declared, *"No!"* and that, *"Christians, of all people, must traffic in the commodity called hope."* He is right. At a time when the world is starving for hope, followers of Jesus, of all the people on earth, are the ones to blaze with hope, for it is they who have tasted the glorious Kingdom to come.

A Final Word

Perhaps you have never given your life to Jesus Christ. Possibly you did once, but today you are far away from him. The Bible declares, *"For all have sinned; all fall short of God's glorious standard"* [4] and adds that the *"wages of sin is death, but the free gift of God is eternal life in Christ Jesus our Lord."* [5] Salvation is the gift of God; you cannot earn it by being good or religious. What does salvation actually mean? It means you will not go to hell because you have broken God's laws, but spend eternity with him, living forever in a new heaven and earth, enjoying the immortality of a resurrection body. Now that is being saved! Jesus promised, *"I am the resurrection and the life. Those who believe in me, even though they die like everyone else, will live again."* [6]

Jesus Christ died on a cross for you. If you believe in him and receive him, he will give you power to become a child of God. The question is where do you stand? *"God has given us eternal life,"* said the Apostle John, *"and this life is in his Son. He who has the Son has life; he who has not the Son of God does not have life. I write this to you who believe in the name of the son of God, that you may know that you have eternal life."* [7]

Salvation is completely dependent on whether you have the Son of God or not. The good news is that you can receive him today. Why delay? If you need to give your life to Christ, or if you have been away from him and need to come back to him, then I invite you to pray this simple prayer and, as you mean it with all your being, God will answer you:

"Lord Jesus, please forgive all my sins. I don't want to be separated from you forever. Lord I want to be with you always. I believe you died for me, that You took the punishment for my sins so that I could be forgiven. Lord Jesus, I receive You. I open the door of my life and ask You come in and take control. Lord, I give You my life. Amen."

If you prayed this prayer, may I suggest that you do the following to help you grow in faith:

- ⁊ Obtain a Bible and start reading it everyday.

- ⁊ Find a good Bible-believing church as soon as you are able, one that will encourage and strengthen you. Make friends with other keen Christians.

- ⁊ Tell people what you have done. It is in openly declaring that you are a follower of Jesus Christ that your salvation is sealed: *"For if you confess with your mouth that Jesus is Lord and believe in your heart that God raised him from the dead, you will be saved."* [8]

And so, as we have come to the end of this journey, my prayer is that you may be like King David of Israel who sang, *"Lord, remind me how brief my time on earth will be. Remind me that my days are numbered, and that my life is fleeing away. And so, Lord, where do I put my hope? My only hope is in you."* [9]

Notes

[1] Sir Winston Churchill (1874-1965), British statesman and Prime Minister of England 1940-45, 1951-55.

[2] Jeremiah 17:7,8

[3] Habakkuk 2:3

[4] Romans 3:23

[5] Romans 6:23

[6] John 11:25

[7] 1 John 5:11-13 (RSV)

8   Romans 10:9
9   Psalm 39:4,7

To contact the author or to order additional copies of *Hope*,
Write: David Peters, c/o Teleios Ministries,
PO Box 58-644, Greenmount,
Auckland, New Zealand

Email: davidp@teleios.org.nz

Website: www.teleios.org.nz